The Gospel According to Cancer

Reflections for Women with Cancer

PATRICIA A. GOULD-CHAMP

FOREWORD BY JOHN W. KINNEY

MMGI BOOKS • CHICAGO

Published by MMGI Books, Chicago, IL 60636
www.mmgibooks.com

The Gospel According to Cancer:
Reflections for Women with Cancer

Copyright © 2014 by Patricia A. Gould-Champ, Richmond, VA 23227

All rights reserved.

No part of this publication may be reproduced, stored in a retrieval system, or transmitted in any form or by any means, electronic, mechanical, photocopying, recording, or otherwise, without the prior permission of the copyright owner, except for brief quotations included in a review of the book.

MMGI Books has made every effort to trace the ownership of quotes. In the event of a question arising from the use of a quote, we regret any error made and will be pleased to make the necessary corrections in future printings and editions of this book.

Bible quotations in this volume designated NIV are from THE HOLY BIBLE: NEW INTERNATIONAL VERSION®. NIV®. Copyright © 1973, 1978, 1984 by Biblica. Scripture quoted by permission. All rights reserved worldwide.

Other Bible quotations throughout are paraphrased.

Library of Congress Cataloging-in-Publication Data

The Gospel According to Cancer: Reflections for Women with Cancer by Patricia A. Gould-Champ

p. cm

ISBN 978-1-939774-08-8 (pbk. : alk. Paper)

Inspirational—Religious life. 2. Motivational—Conduct of life. 3. Healing—Empowerment of life.

Printed in the U.S.A.

Sisters Network Central Virginia, Inc., one of the 40-plus affiliate chapters of Sisters Network® Inc. (SNI), has partnered with Dr. Patricia Gould-Champ to Stop the Silence®. She gives voice to many survivors. She brings hope through sharing her personal testimonies and offers support and commitment to activate change in attitude and actions for the ultimate success in our mission. We proudly endorse this book as it will inspire so many Sisters to push forward and push through. We believe "We can do all things through Christ who strengthens us"! For additional information on Sisters Network Central Virginia, Inc., please visit our local website www.sistersnetworkcentralva.org or our national website www.sistersnetworkinc.org.

Brenda Archer
President
Sisters Network Central Virginia, Inc.

The Gospel According to Cancer is a resource for the soul of every woman. Through laughter and tears from meditation titles to text, the subject of cancer becomes a vehicle that ushers us down paths of vulnerability and strength; grief and celebration; utter anger, disappointment, and deep love—paths that we all must travel. I could not put the book down! Patricia Gould-Champ rushed me by the destabilizing facts of cancer, delivering me to wonderful truths and prayers of freedom and the peace of knowing and unknowing. I accepted invitations to be comfortable with the vulnerable and the beautiful, the strong and nowhere-near strong; and ultimately received a challenge to love myself enough to care for myself.

Dr. Alison Gise Johnson
Director, Doctor of Ministry Program
Samuel DeWitt Proctor School of Theology, Virginia Union University

In these meditations, Pastor Patricia Gould-Champ shares her intimate and personal journey through cancer, but amazingly so, she speaks for those of us, both male and female, who have made that journey with our loved ones. Packed with words that elicit both tears and laughter, she pulls the reader into her journey, whether they are ready to come or not. With personal vulnerability and spiritual audacity, she empowers each of us to live our lives to the fullest and trust the God who gave us life in the first place.

Dr. Mary H. Young
Assistant Professor of Christian Education and Director of the MACE Program
Samuel DeWitt Proctor School of Theology, Virginia Union University

The Gospel According to Cancer is a stimulating work that will enable its readers to marinate on its collection of inspirational, enriching, and edifying moments along Dr. Gould-Champ's journey. The work reflects the strength of the human spirit and psyche during some of the most daunting times in life. I highly recommend this wonderful book as a means to inspire, educate, and encourage weary souls on this sometimes tumultuous journey called life.

Delegate Delores L. McQuinn
Representative, 70th House District
Commonwealth of Virginia

There is no "Hollywood" concept to this script. It is pure personal experience between Pat, God, family, and others in her social circle of life. It is both "personal" and "personable." It is a script that is refreshing without a lot of "philosophical quips." This script will make you think seriously about your life and cause you to answer the question "Where will my help come from?" Be glad to have this testimony in your possession. Be blessed by the spiritual "uplift" it shares and share the blessing with others. God blesses us in varied ways; this is one of those ways.

Dr. Robert L. Pettis, Sr.
Senior Pastor
Zion Baptist Church, Richmond, Virginia

Family members of women living with and through cancer (on the "cancer journey") will have their eyes opened and their hearts touched by the wisdom Dr. Gould-Champ shares with the reader. Women who have been diagnosed with cancer will feel as if Dr. Gould-Champ is telling their story as they read each truthful page. People of faith will laugh with her, cry with her, think through difficult passages with her, and pray with her as she prays for them and puts into words prayers too deep for the tongue to utter. I recommend her work to all who are searching for answers and searching for God in the midst of their journey. You will be blessed by the way God has blessed her.

Rev. Dr. Jeremiah A. Wright, Jr.
Pastor Emeritus
Trinity UCC, Chicago, Illinois

*This book is dedicated to
Champ and Pamela,
who lovingly joined me on the journey.*

Contents

Foreword by John W. Kinney, PhD	xi
Acknowledgments	xiii
Introduction	xvii

The Gospel ACCORDING TO CANCER — 1

It's Cancer	7
What Did I Do Wrong?	8
Living with the Unknown	10
Speaking the Word Cancer	12
Dealing with the Process	13
This Hair Thing	15
How Do I Tell Pamela?	17
Don't Pity Me	19
Life Goes On	20
You're So Strong	22
Where Can I Hide?	23
I'm Tired	25
You Look Beautiful	27
I Don't Feel Like Praying	28
When Panic Sets In	30
Do I Want to Live?	32
On a Scale from 1–10	33
Can I Trust My Doctor?	34
But This is My Body	36
Letting Go	38

Possibility FAITH — 41

A Surgery Date	46
God, I See You	47
I Can't Fix This	48
Prayer Warriors	49
Cancer Doesn't Make It Better	51
The Dishes Still Have to Be Washed	52
Me Time	53
Ain't I a Woman?	55
Chemotherapy	56
Thank God for Family	58
Try This . . .	60
My Testimony	61
The Prayers of the Saints	63
The Class Reunion	65
I Don't See Death When I Look at You	67
The Comfort of Friends	68
When Everyone Else Sleeps	70
The Pastor's Call	71
Radiation	72
Trading Places	74

Against All Odds ...I WILL NOT DIE BUT LIVE   77

A Mother's Love	90
Being a Patient	91
Another Birthday	92
Barry Died!	94
Being Loved Again	96
It's Not Over	97
Anticlimactic	99
Daring to Grieve	100
Accepting the Changes	102
Preaching through the Storm	103
My Daddy's Strength	105
Living without Fear	106
A Sense of Humor	108
As Normal as It Gets	109
Joining My Sisters	111
Another Chance	112
Survivor or Conqueror?	114
5 Years!	115
What Will Be My Legacy?	116
I Plan to Live Until I Die!	118

Foreword

Christian theology and proclamation have often been criticized for being disconnected reflections devoid of primary experience. Dr. Gould-Champ recovers the soul of preaching and testimony grounded in the fiber of flux of life. In recent years, there has been a slipping away of faith into the deluded realm of triumphalized and romanticized religiosity. In this realm, we are led to believe that the faithful are immune and/or excused from the "troubles of this world." This religion suggests that any encounter with trials, tears, and travails indicates a failure in your faith or a lack of spiritual discipline and depth. True believers, as they move through the twists and turns of authentic existence, are wounded and burdened by this brand of religion.

Dr. Gould-Champ leads us out of simplistic and shallow faith and provides us with a window to her soul and her deep faith as she recounts her confrontation with the diagnosis that causes us to tremble. With deep spirit, clear thought, unfailing faith, and flowing pen, she shares her journey "through" cancer and the attending fear, guilt, confusion, pain, and struggle. With grit, grace, and growth, she lifts the veil of a crisis that dims the future and allows us to see and experience the presence and the promise in every circumstance.

Her testimony is ontically constructed and powerfully communicated as we discover that illumination can be experienced in the deepest darkness and strength can be realized in broken places. In the "valley," existence is turned inside out, essence is discovered, a light comes on, and the valley and mountaintop meet. No diagnosis or prognosis can mute the good news, and in deep agony we discover a deeper self and a greater God. Dr. Gould-Champ reminds us that, even when negative circumstances attempt to distort and determine us, we can meet the essential, beautiful self who is defined by neither hair nor breasts nor other body parts.

Pat writes from the experience of a woman and in the voice of a woman, but, in so doing, she touches the humanity and the divinity of all of us. We all must walk by faith! This faith does not destroy sight but rather extends our sight beyond the limited constructions accessed only by our senses. This faith does not eliminate all fear, but it does strip fear of the authority to remove our joy, diminish our hope, shape our attitude, and determine our destiny. In this faith, God is real, life is celebrated, the soul sings "yes," and glory grasps us!

Whenever and wherever God "shows up" we find ourselves praising God. God "shows up" in *The Gospel According to Cancer* and I say "Hallelujah!"

John W. Kinney, PhD
Samuel DeWitt Proctor School of Theology, Virginia Union University

Acknowledgments

This book is the result of the love of an amazing God and the support of a wonderful group of family, friends, and colleagues. There are so many people who assisted in bringing this project to completion, too many to name. But I am grateful to them all.

I am grateful to those who were instrumental in my physical healing. I was blessed to be treated at the Massey Cancer Center, the Virginia Commonwealth University Health System (MCV) in Richmond, Virginia. My team of doctors, Dr. Harry Bear and Dr. Mary Jo Hackney, were wonderful. They along with the many doctors, nurses, and technicians displayed a special brand of extreme kindness and patience that was critical to my healing. My treatment there was first-rate and a model of healing ministry at its finest.

I am grateful to my colleagues at the Samuel DeWitt Proctor School of Theology who urged me write. I thank Dean John W. Kinney for his gentle prodding and for Dr. Alison Gise Johnson, Dr. Adam Bond, Dr. Mary Young, and Dr. Katie Cannon who assured me that this work was worthy of print. I thank my big brother in ministry, Dr. Robert Pettis, who lovingly first called my meditations "the gospel according to cancer." I am grateful for those who read the meditations and were kind enough to offer words of endorsement.

I am grateful to my church family at Faith Community Baptist Church for their love and commitment to the work of ministry for the past nineteen years. Their constant faith has been a model for me and encouraged me to share these meditations with the wider community of faith. They walked with me during the entire course of this medical ordeal and held my arms up on every occasion. Without their love and support, our family would have found this journey unbearable. I am thankful to God for our walk together as a church family.

My family has been awesome. I am a product of the awesome legacy of James William and Dorothy Coles Gould. Their love and strength along with that of my deceased brother, Dexter Gould, Sr., have been my inspiration throughout this ordeal. Their faith has sustained me in times of weakness. My aunt and cousin, Doris and Cheryl Davis, who are more like sisters, have been there to assist in every way possible. My beloved nephew, DJ, and his mother, Carolyn, gave me a package of healing scriptures and music to soothe my soul. The love and prayers of my extended family and friends throughout the country have been a source of encouragement.

For all of my sister-survivors who shared their stories of triumph and encouraged me along the way, this book is written to honor them. I am especially thankful to my mother-in-law, Mrs. Delois Champ, for her constant reassurance. I pray that this work can be of benefit to the work of the Sisters Network Central Virginia, Inc. and can be a source of encouragement and strength to the thousands of women who are diagnosed with breast cancer each day. My prayers are with them and their families.

I am thankful to Rev. Darryl Sims and the staff of MMGI Books for the love they have given to preparing this book for publication. When I first spoke with Dr. Sims, he was excited about what this work meant to me and what my vision was for sharing it with others. He has been careful to maintain the integrity of my offering and for that I am eternally grateful. It was a pleasure to work with him and I thank him for his assistance and guidance.

Finally, this book could not and would not have come into being without the love of my husband, Champ, and our daughter, Pamela, who lovingly joined me on the journey. They have journeyed with me during my walk with cancer and shared in every aspect, from the deepest of sorrows to the highest of joys. I thank them for loving me to life.

Introduction

At the tender age of seven as I sat with one of the mothers of the church while my mother sang in the choir, I accepted Jesus Christ as my Lord and Savior. That one decision has led to 60 years of experiencing the awesome joy of being in relationship with the Lord. Like most people who were saved as children, my faith has grown and matured through the years. My faith has allowed me to share every aspect of my life with the Lord—the good, the bad, and the ugly. From childhood, my faith has been my source of strength and my comfort in times of trouble. My faith has seen me through time and time again. Therefore, when I was confronted with the diagnosis of cancer, I turned to my faith to guide me through.

In November 2003, I was diagnosed with stage-three breast cancer and it sent me on a journey that would forever change my life. This journey included, but was not limited to, two bouts of chemotherapy, a mastectomy, and radiation therapy. From the day I received the initial news and throughout every aspect of my cancer journal, I had to walk by faith and not by sight. My cancer diagnosis was devastating. The range of feelings were so intense they stunned me and left me emotionally and spiritually drained. I decided that I needed to get the feeling out of my head and out of my heart and in a place where God could deal with me and with what I was going through.

With the exception of my mother-in-law, I had not talked with any other women who had cancer. My mother-in-law, who was a 20-year survivor, was wonderful in sharing her story. She encouraged me to trust the new medicine and treatments that had become available since her diagnosis. She was a blessing to me, but her journey was not my journey. It was after talking with her that I wrote the first "cancer" entry into my journal. I felt I had to get down on paper how I felt when I first received the news. I needed to lay my raw feelings before the God who knew me, understood me, and loved me. I knew that God would allow me to be honest as I revealed my faith struggles on a daily basis.

I decided to use my journaling as a therapeutic tool during my cancer journey. It seemed that once I started writing, I could not stop. My journaling became like prayer. I've always believed that praying without ceasing is about living a life of prayer—a life that keeps you in constant communication and contact with God, every moment, every conscious second of your life. This life of prayer is sharing with God everything that happens on a daily basis. So faithfully, every week I would reflect on what God was doing or had done and I would commit it to paper. It was special prayer as I poured out my heart and soul before God in my journal. I was amazed at how the bad news of cancer was turned into "good news" as God gradually healed my body, heart, and soul.

These meditations represent a span of five years. They cover a wide range of topics, all as the Spirit directed. As I began to read them, I found myself amazed to see how many topics had been covered and how candid I had been able to be. My journal entries are so personal, and I never imagined that I would share them with anyone. But the Lord had something else in mind. I first shared a few when I revealed my status to the church where I serve as pastor, and then I shared them with a few persons who had received a cancer diagnosis. Over and over, people shared how the meditations had touched them emotionally, inspired them to not give up, and encouraged them to walk by faith and not by sight. But it took quite a while for these meditations to become *The Gospel According to Cancer*.

As I began to speak to women's cancer awareness groups, I was increasingly asked to share more and more of my journal writings. People began to ask if they could have copies or inquire where they could find the book. As I struggled with putting my emotional self out there for all to see, I was encouraged by my colleagues to write the book. After one of my dear friends died of cancer, I began to finally yield to the idea of publishing these meditations. Once I was finally committed to putting my meditations into book form, I started with a pretty solid title: *By Faith and Not by Sight: Reflections for Women with Cancer*. But a chance conversation with a "big brother" changed the title and resolved any issues I had with revealing the full experience of my cancer journey. After listening to me talk about the content of the meditations for the book, he simply said to me: *hmmm . . . the gospel according to cancer*. It went straight to my heart, led me to preach the sermon *The Gospel According to Cancer*, and caused me to retitle the book.

Many people have been intrigued by the title of this book. For many the paring of the word *gospel* with the word *cancer* seems an oxymoron. But for me, the gospel or good news concerning the saving power of Jesus Christ is revealed and found relevant on a daily basis as we endure all of life's situations. In fact, it is in the midst of trouble and tribulation that God shows up strong and gives us victorious good news. Scripture reveals this by reminding us that *neither death nor life . . . nor any powers, neither height nor depth . . . will be able to separate us from the love of God that is in Christ Jesus our Lord*. The gospel is continuing to be written by every situation that we experience. The gospel according to cancer is a reflection of what cancer has revealed about the constant and abiding love of God in Christ Jesus.

The Gospel According to Cancer consists of sixty meditations and three sermons. This book is a five-year testimony of the power of God to shepherd us through the most difficult situations with grace, laughter, and peace. These meditations have caused me to cry, laugh, shout, and sit in complete silence before the Lord. These meditations represent my offerings to those who need encouragement and hope in the midst of the seemingly "bad news" of cancer and other tragic situations. These meditations reveal the power of God to lift our spirits and give us new hope for each new day.

My prayers will be with you as you read these meditations. I pray that they will minister to you, challenge you to see God in what you're going through, and encourage you to walk by faith and not by sight. I hope that you will share not only these meditations with others, but, most of all, I hope that *The Gospel According to Cancer* will inspire you to share your own testimony of faith that even in the midst of the cancer, or whatever you're going through, God can and will provide some "good news." As you read this book, I pray that God will do for you what God did for me—heal you from the inside out.

Patricia A. Gould-Champ

The Gospel According to Cancer

For I am convinced that neither death nor life, neither angels nor demons, neither the present nor the future, nor any powers, neither height nor depth, nor anything else in all creation, will be able to separate us from the love of God that is in Christ Jesus our Lord.
ROMANS 8:38-39, NIV

My sermon today is *The Gospel According to Cancer* . . . the gospel according to *my money ain't right*; the gospel according to *things ain't right in my life*; the gospel according to *my man left*; the gospel according to *my woman left*; the gospel according to *my car won't start*; the gospel according to *I ain't got no job*; the gospel according to *whatever is going wrong in your life*. That's what I want to preach about today. I don't know about anybody else, but I need this word.

I'm sure that when some of you read it in the bulletin, your first reaction was—*Preacher, are you crazy?* That was certainly my reaction when God shared this message with me to give to you because for most of us, cancer is a death sentence. Just the word *cancer* strikes fear in our hearts and often robs us of our confidence and sometimes even our faith. But what God wants all of us to know today is that it is possible for cancer to be the catalyst to strengthen our faith and to reveal Jesus Christ to us in ways that we could not receive before. In the midst of the cancers of this life—and there are many other cancerous situations that we face on a daily basis—cancer in our body, cancer in our finances, cancer in our relationships—whatever the cancer we face, there is still some good news. The gospel is the good news concerning the life, death, and resurrection of Jesus Christ. The gospel is the good news that because Jesus Christ died and rose again there is some keeping power for you and for me, in spite of what we have to face in this life.

In our text for today, Paul is writing to those who need encouragement. The Book of Romans is a very personal letter to people who, like us, are under the burdens of daily living. Paul himself is a witness to how life can deal you some bad news and how life does not always give you what you feel you deserve. But Paul has lived a life of faith that has taught him that nothing in this life, *neither life nor death, hardships or tribulations, will be able to separate him from the love of God that is in Christ Jesus.* I don't know about you but that's some mighty "good news." And today, God is inviting all of us in whatever state we find ourselves to receive the good news of God's saving grace. Today there is still some good news, good news for cancer survivors, good news for those who made it to see another day, good news for those of us who are still pressing our way. Today there is good news, the gospel according to cancer, whatever that cancer is—the good news is that God still loves us and God's grace is still sufficient!

Cancer and other such problems teach us a lot about God. In the final analysis, it's not about cancer—it's about God. And the gospel according to cancer first declares that **there is good news in spite of the diagnosis**. Sometimes we are destroyed by the diagnosis. There have been studies where people who were perfectly well were told they were seriously ill, and they allowed the diagnosis to literally make them ill and some died. This happens in life all the time—when we receive the bad news that life gives us we immediately begin to lose all hope. But Paul encourages the people by saying it does not matter, *because in all things God works for the good of those who love God and have been called according to God's purpose.* In other words, even after we receive the worst of news, God is able to work on our behalf. God does God's best work not always before the diagnosis but after the diagnosis. The good news according to cancer is that when cancer came, God stepped in and began to do what only God could do. Today, in spite of the diagnosis, in spite of what life says, in spite of what your situation says, in spite of what doctors say, in spite of what you see or don't see, there is still some good news. And that good news is that God is a way-maker and God is available and God's love is sufficient to keep us in perfect peace. Yes, there is still some good news; there is always some good news in spite of the diagnosis.

Anyone get a bad diagnosis? A bad diagnosis at the doctor's office, a bad diagnosis on the job, a bad diagnosis with regard to a relationship, a bad diagnosis at the bank—it sounds like death; it feels like it's not going to work out. But God is calling us to hear the good news because, in spite of it all, our God has a different report. Whose report are we going to believe? Will we believe the report of the enemy? Will we believe the report of the world? Or will we believe the report of the gospel—the good report, the good news of the Lord?

Cancer is a journey—a hard journey. But the gospel according to cancer teaches us that **there is good news in spite of the journey**. In this life, the journey can be full of our own personal cancers—those things that threaten to kill and destroy us physically, mentally, emotionally, economically, and even spiritually. But we serve a God who is with us on the journey. This journey called life is both a common journey and a personal journey. While we go through some of the same things, it's personal and different for each of us. Although I can share what I experienced as a cancer survivor, it's different and unique for each person. But the good news is that God is with us all. No matter how rough, no matter how life deals with us, no matter what answers we have, no matter what answers we will never have—God is with us on the journey, working it out for our good.

All of us are on our own personal journey. And our journey can be exhausting and painful and fearful and full of anxiety, but we have to keep traveling. All of us in here today have our own set of problems and issues that we have to face as we move to the next level in this life. And sometimes, for all of our trying, we are left feeling overwhelmed and defeated. But Paul reminds us that there is still some good news in spite of what this journey puts in our path. Paul reminds us that the Spirit is available to walk with us on this journey—we don't have to do life by ourselves. The Spirit is our power source—we can walk by faith and not by sight.

Life is a journey that is full of surprises. Just when we think we have it all figured out, life throws something in our path. There's always some stumbling block, some unexpected obstacle. And sometimes the journey becomes overwhelming, but we forget that it's the journey that gets us there. It's on the journey that we come to know who God really is. It's on the journey, with its ups and downs, its misfortune and sickness and trials and tribulations, this journey where sometimes our hearts are broken and our hopes are dashed, it's on the journey where we meet God and where we see God move and we see God's power and grace and mercy. It's on this journey that we receive the good news that Jesus hung, bled, and died, but he got up so that each and every day we can still have joy, still have good news in spite of what we encounter on the journey.

Some news causes you to focus on the end result in a negative way. Cancer is like that—most illness is like that. We immediately begin to focus on a negative end. And even if we don't focus on a negative end, we begin to focus on what we desire the outcome to be. But as believers who walk by faith and not by sight, God promises us good news in spite of the outcome. The gospel according to cancer is that **there is good news in spite of the outcome**. Many cancer survivors have come to believe that. Paul, who had survived some of life's hard situations, had come to believe that; and while in a prison cell, he shares some encouraging words with those he loves. He wanted them to know that they have to look beyond how it appeared—they had to look beyond the prison walls that held him captive and know that there would be good news in spite of the outcome.

Healing is God's work, and God is in the healing business. Healing is God's divine outcome for those whom God loves. Paul says we all face death on a daily basis, but by the grace of Almighty God we are more than conquerors. Paul says that in spite of the diagnosis that life gives us and the things that we face along the journey of life, none of that has the power to separate us from God's love.

God's love is healing. Without God's love no real healing can ever take place. God's love keeps us in perfect peace. Healing on this side without God's love means nothing because when we are separated from God's love, that is what death is. But the good news is that we serve a God who promises to never leave us nor forsake us. Whatever we go through, God is able to meet us at the point of every need. So we don't have to worry about the outcome, it's all good. On this side or on the other side, it's all good because nothing can separate us from the love of God who has all power. It's all good because the love of God knows just what we stand in need of, and the love of God can do anything but fail!

There's some mighty good news—good news of the gospel of Jesus Christ. This good news came from the very heart of God, the God who made Heaven and Earth, the only true and living God. Before God created us, he knew that in this life we would have many troubles. He knew that in this life there would be sickness and hardship and that trouble would come. God knew that we would have to cry sometimes. God knew that that cancer would come. And God knew that we would need some good news in spite of it all. So God sent his only Son, Jesus, and allowed him to die on an old rugged cross outside the city gates. But on the third day, early on a Sunday morning, God raised Jesus from the grave. And now, at the name of Jesus, every knee shall bow and every tongue shall confess.

Now there is some eternal good news—in spite of the diagnosis, in spite of the journey, and in spite of outcome. The good news is that God is with us. The good news is that God is keeping us. There's good news in spite of cancer, good news in the midnight hours, good news in the hospital, good news in the courtroom, good news early in the morning, good news to those who need healing, good news for those of us who love God. *Who shall separate us from the love of Christ? Shall tribulation, or distress, or persecution, or famine, or nakedness, or peril, or sword, or cancer? No, nothing—nothing—NOTHING. WE ARE MORE THAN CONQUERORS!*

It's Cancer

HELLO, MRS. GOULD-CHAMP, I GOT YOUR LAB WORK BACK AND IT'S CANCER.

I don't know if there is any good way to receive that kind of news. I sat on the bed waiting for some buildup, some gentle easing into the news I had been dreading to hear for about two weeks. And in a second—so matter-of-factly—I get it—right between the eyes. *It's cancer.* As I sat on the bed, I really couldn't digest the rest of the conversation. I remember only bits and pieces. *We will need to take another mammogram—we don't want the cancer to return—we'll try to do surgery as soon as we can—chemotherapy—I'll need to see you next week.*

Wait, stop, can we go back and take it in slow motion? Can I have a minute to prepare myself? You're taking my breath away. It's too much—it's too soon. I need more time.

As a woman, it's hard to come face to face with the fact that you're mortal. Oh, of course we know that we are, but in most instances we act as if we will indeed live forever and we will be able to do what we do forever. We ignore our body—it tries to talk to us but we won't listen. My body tried to tell me it was cancer months before I decided to make the appointment. My body had begged me to stop ignoring that hard place on my right breast. But I was too busy. After all, I was caring for a sick mother after the death of my father. I'll check on myself later. There's plenty of time—I'm indispensable. But now I have to listen. *It's cancer.*

It's cancer. My mind goes through a range of emotions. I'm angry at a doctor who would dare to call and tell me such news over the phone. What's wrong with him? Why couldn't he set an appointment and tell me in the "comfort" of his office? I'm angry at myself for thinking that I could neglect this body and ignore the consequences of that neglect. I'm angry because I don't have time to be sick. I am a care-provider—I don't have time to be sick! God,

I am not too pleased with you right now because this is the worst possible time for me to be sick. I'm angry! I'm afraid—I don't know how to be sick. I've sat through countless appointments with my parents—listening to doctors—administering medication—but *I don't know how to be sick.* I don't know how to be vulnerable.

It's cancer. These are words that can't be taken back. These are words that change a normal day into the beginning of a journey into the unknown. These are words that test who you are and what you believe and what faith really is. So I take a moment to cry. I cry for me and for what can never be again. I cry and I give thanks to God for today. And then I get up and I go into the kitchen and I say to the man to whom I've been married for eighteen years—*It's cancer.* And I watch the tears well up in his eyes and we hold each other and know that the journey has begun. Today we begin the journey and we commit ourselves to walk *by faith and not by sight.*

Dear Lord, bless all of my sisters who have just been told that it's cancer. Lord, you know the fear and the helplessness we feel. But in spite of the news, we know that you are an awesome God who has power to heal us and to make us whole. We trust you and even now we place ourselves in your hands. Keep us, guide us, and fulfill your promises in our lives. Amen.

What Did I Do Wrong?

GUILT IS A TERRIBLE THING. Whenever something bad happens in our lives, guilt comes and takes a seat and demands our attention. One of the first questions I asked when I was diagnosed with cancer was, *what did I do wrong?* And I asked the question because I was pretty sure that I had the answer. I was way too large—I had gained so much weight in the last ten years. I ate too much of the wrong food. I didn't do enough exercise. I had been a smoker in my young adult years. I missed two years of mammograms. I could go on and on. Surely, all of this is my fault.

In the days and weeks after finding out I had cancer, I took my emotional boxing gloves out and I went to town on myself. All of the bad choices and neglectful behavior that I thought could have contributed to my condition, I used to beat myself up day and night nonstop. I couldn't talk about it to my husband, but I tried to detect glimpses of accusation in his eyes. Guilt had me going. I needed somewhere to place the blame—I needed a reason for this to happen. I needed to take the responsibility for this sickness and so I lingered with the question, *what did I do wrong?*

This challenge was one of the first hurdles of my sickness. It's amazing how we say one thing but we live another. It's amazing how faith sounds when we're sick as opposed to when we're well. When we're well, we seem to understand that God is in control of all things. When we're well, we seem to understand that God is not the author of sickness and pain. When we're well, we seem to know and encourage others to understand that God does not use pain and suffering to get back at us for our mistakes and bad choices. But when we're sick, it doesn't matter how long we've walked with God or how well we know these things, our thinking changes. It's a test of faith. Sickness causes you to doubt—to doubt things that you know and have lived and walked all of your life. Sickness will cause you to entertain thoughts that you would never have given a moment's notice when you were well. Sickness will cause a woman who has walked by faith all of her life, and who had declared on more than one occasion that *without faith it is impossible to please God*, to entertain the thought that what she did or did not do resulted in this dreadful disease.

What did I do wrong? You lived, and life is full of surprises, both good and bad. Life is full of sickness and pain and suffering and we are not exempt. What we could have done or should have done or needed to have done has nothing to do with having cancer. Cancer is not of God; cancer is not God's plan for any of us. Yes, we have cancer, but cancer does not override God's grace and God's mercy. Let us let go of the whys and the what ifs and spend our valuable time with the God who promises to comfort us and meet us at the point of every need.

Dear Lord, as women, we often blame ourselves for everything bad that happens in our lives. Thank you for moving us past the blame game. Mother God, thank you for helping us to let go and allow your grace and mercy to comfort us. Keep us ever in your care. Amen.

Living with the Unknown

CANCER IS THE UNKNOWN. I have never had cancer before and it represents the scary unknown. When I was first diagnosed, all of the nurses and people I would talk to used a similar phase when referring to cancer: *It's a journey.* For me their words were shrouded in secrecy and mystery. If cancer is a journey, it was a journey into the unknown and a journey that I dreaded. I don't like living with the unknown.

How do you live with the unknown? To be sure, life is unknown. We never know what each new day holds. We live by trusting God to reveal the mysteries of life to us day by day. The unknown journey of life becomes palatable because of a God whom we know and who knows us. Even though we quest to know all about this journey called life, it is actually the mystery and the not knowing that keeps us from losing our minds. If we knew what lies ahead, many of us would give up and not have the courage to take the next tiny steps forward. In actuality, we're already living with the unknown.

Cancer makes life uncertain in ways that we find hard to explain. Things that we used to take for granted, we no longer can. Things that we assumed would continue or would never end now become questionable. We look at things differently. Calendars lose their power over our lives. Now we are mindful that our plans are nothing. We are living with the unknown. And this unknown journey does not bow down to our plans or to our desires.

I remember being frozen in time, afraid to make any plans. I remember those beginning days when I was first diagnosed. I cleared my calendar and was afraid to place any new engagements on it. I couldn't tell anyone why but I felt that because I didn't know what tomorrow held that I couldn't plan for tomorrow. Living with the unknown had caused me to assume that because I didn't know and couldn't control what would happen tomorrow that I could cease to live with hope.

Living with the unknown is one of the givens of life. We never know what tomorrow holds. But we know the One who holds tomorrow. And because of our knowledge of a God who gives us power for living, we can still make plans. The hope of our God is that even in the midst of the uncertainties of life, we still make plans. We still anticipate the graciousness of a God who moves us beyond our present situation. So, even with cancer, I began to put things on my calendar. Even with cancer, I will live with expectation and with hope and with a sense of seeing what lies ahead. This is the mystery of faith that allows us to not grieve as those who have no hope. *Now faith is being sure of what we hope for and certain of what we do not see.* With this in mind, I can live with the unknown.

Dear Lord, thank you for your presence during this time in our lives. Help us as we struggle to understand this new uncertainty. Lord, we need to know that you will be with us. Bless every moment and reveal yourself at each new dawn. Help us to know you better and to trust you more. Amen.

Speaking the Word Cancer

WORDS HAVE POWER. And the word cancer is a powerful word. The word cancer can strike fear in the hearts of even the strongest of women. When the doctor said *it's cancer*, my heart skipped a beat. The words took the breath out of me. It attacked my spirit and for a brief, fleeting moment, I thought that I would surely die.

I don't know what others hear when they hear the word cancer but for me the word cancer meant death. For me the initial announcement that I had cancer was tantamount to receiving a death sentence. I heard the word but my mind refused to receive the word. For weeks, I could not say the word cancer. I talked all around the word. But the word could not, would not come out of my mouth. Somehow I felt that to speak the word was to give in to what I perceived was its power over my life. If I just don't say the word, it will cease to be cancer. If I don't say the word, it will go away and I will be instantly healed. So for three weeks, the word cancer lingered in the air. Except for when I shared the diagnosis with my husband, I did not speak it to anyone.

It's amazing how God allows us to break the power of fear in our lives. In praying for another, I asked, as is my custom, *what do you want me to pray for?* And they told me in detail of their concern. I then proceeded to pray with the same detail for their healing and deliverance. The revelation of the moment did not come immediately. But a few days later as I remembered that prayer, the Spirit of God spoke to remind me that we have to name our need. Cancer cannot be healed if it remains in the region of the unspoken.

Jesus always asked people, *what do you want?* Of course he already knew, but he needed them to speak it, to acknowledge the need in their lives. Speaking the word cancer is not a sign of defeat but a sign of faith. It signals that we trust in a God who can take the power out of words like cancer and death. Our God allows us to say it knowing that by speaking the word it releases God's healing power.

My release came slowly. It was not a planned event. One day, the Spirit of God stood up and I declared very calmly, *I have cancer.* There, I've said it. The yoke is broken. It's a word, a condition—not my master. We are not bound by the world's statistics. We are cared for by a God who blesses us against all odds. I speak the word cancer so that my God knows exactly what healing I need. Each time I say the word cancer, it becomes less frightening and less intimidating. Each time I speak the word cancer I realize more and more what it cannot do. Each time I speak the word cancer, I realize that it cannot keep me from being healed.

Dear Lord, thank you for your empowering Spirit that sets us free from the bondage of fear. Lord, thank you for each new day that moves us closer to owning your healing in our lives. Today we claim life and not death. Today we claim joy and not fear. The power for living is in your presence. Amen.

Dealing with the Process

SOMEONE ONCE SAID, IF THE CANCER DOESN'T KILL YOU, THE PROCESS WILL. Frustration is the only way to describe the process of my cancer treatment. The process is confusing, frustrating, agitating, tiring, intimidating, and draining. The first week, I felt like giving up. There was too much to remember, too many things coming at me at once, and way too much information that didn't make sense. There were lost charts and being shuffled from one doctor's office to the next and from one lab to the next. There were phone calls that I felt weren't returned quickly enough. Don't these people understand that I have cancer? Don't they know that I need everything to stop and for them to give me their undivided attention? Don't they know that I need to be treated as if I am their one and only patient?

Dealing with the process will be one of the most difficult things to handle. I was a person used to getting responses when I asked for them. I was used to quick turnarounds when problems needed to be solved. Basically, I was used to being in charge. But this process would not allow me to be in charge. It paid me no attention whatsoever. It seemed as if things dragged on and on. People got back to me when they felt like it, or so I felt. And I found it hard to deal with repeating the same information over and over. No matter who I saw, I had to start all over again with the same information. I wanted to scream, *do you people read charts?* Every doctor, every technician, every visit—the same questions, the same information had to be given. This cancer treatment is making me sick and I haven't even gotten started.

As I shared my frustration with the process, it moved my husband to the limit. He was on the verge of reporting doctors for unprofessional conduct because of lost records. He was on the phone demanding answers and pushing the process through. The frustration of the process coupled with his mounting frustration and my fragile emotional state caused for a horrible month. Every day was an endless barrage of phone calls and office visits. We finally had to conclude that we probably needed to be at another facility that could better meet our needs and maintain our confidence. With the help of friends in the medical field, we were able to make the transition. Just getting to that conclusion was a process in and of itself.

With the transition to a new facility, the process started all over again. Was it easy? NO. The process is the process. No matter what we are going through, we have to adhere to the process. Our healing is a process—a process that is not easily tolerated. But unfortunately, we cannot bypass any part of the process. For it is in the process that God does God's best work. In this cancer treatment process I've learned so many things. I've learned to be patient and to be tolerant. I've learned to be understanding of others. I've learned to trust the process and the God of the process. It is in the process that we see God move and God reminds us that our healing is ultimately God's work. So I had to back up and submit—yes, SUBMIT—to the process. And once I did, I was able to allow my healing to begin.

Dear Lord, thank you for being in this process with us. Without your divine presence we could not make it. Thank you for pushing us forward and for pulling us when we want to linger behind. Keep loving us into the next stage of our healing. We bless your marvelous name! Amen.

This Hair Thing

HAIR IS VERY IMPORTANT TO WOMEN. For the African American woman, it's a critical part of who we are. As a black woman, hair has been a personal struggle all of my life. I've struggled with hairstyles. I struggled for a year with whether to dye my rapidly turning gray hair until I finally decided to allow nature to take its course. I've struggled with long hair versus short hair, natural hair versus straightened or permed hair. This hair thing has been a struggle. But finally at 58 years old, I had reached a point of satisfaction with my hair. When I looked in the mirror and saw my beautiful silver-gray, short crown of hair, I was pleased. So when I heard that one of the side effects of my treatment for cancer would be the loss of my hair, I was devastated.

I'm going to lose my hair. I had to sit with that truth for a moment, but eventually, like everything about my treatment, I had to accept it as one of the givens of having cancer. So in anticipation of losing my hair, I went shopping for a wig. I toyed with the idea of letting my imagination run wild and choosing a style that was radically different from my own. Why not be Tina Turner for a while? Or perhaps try some braids or even dreds? Why not go blond? But of course I finally chose a wig that looked very much like my own hairstyle. The gray mix was perfect and I liked it so much that I purchased two—just in case I needed them.

My hair took forever to come out. They said I would lose it fifteen days after my first chemo treatment. It was actually about a month and a half. And the process was slow. It began to thin but if I combed it a certain way, it still looked full. Then it began to come out when I combed it—the comb would be full of hair. At this point, I began to comb my hair straight back and put a little gel on it and it just looked like another hairstyle. Finally I became impatient and I began to pull it out. Just a gentle tug was all it took for a handful of hair to come out. Over the month, my hair had gotten thinner and thinner and more and more of it had come out or been pulled out. It was decision time. As I sat down one Saturday night, I took a long look at my almost bald head. I had two beautiful wigs on stands waiting to be worn. So in anticipation of wearing one of them to church tomorrow, I washed my hair and allowed the rest of my hair to come out.

As I sat before the mirror on that Sunday morning with full make-up on, I reached over to do the final act of putting on the beautiful mixed-gray wig I had purchased. But as my hand reached out to put it on, I withdrew and looked instead at the woman who stared back at me from the mirror. This was a woman who had learned to be comfortable in her own skin. This was a woman who was surprisingly beautiful with no hair. This was a woman who desired to be free—free of hair and free of the opinions of others. So I smiled back at this woman whom God had created to be beautiful from the inside out. In that instant I discovered the woman God had been trying to reveal to me all of my life—a woman who is more than hair and breasts. I discovered that I not only like, but I love this woman that God has made. So I took one last look, smiled, and went to church with my beautiful, bald self.

Dear Lord, thank you for making us beautiful with or without hair. Thank you for making us women out of your own Spirit. Thank you for giving us choices and options with regard to how we look. May your divine beauty shine forth in our lives day by day. Amen.

How Do I Tell Pamela?

HOW DO I TELL PAMELA? When you have a fifteen-year-old and you've just been told that you have cancer, that's one of the first questions that comes to your mind. How does a mother tell a teenage daughter that she has a disease that may rob her of a mother's presence at a critical time in her life? How do you invade that innocent, carefree time that is a teenager's right and hand them news that will force them to deal with life in ways they could never imagine? One of the pains of having cancer is having to share that news with those you love most.

It was November when we received the news, so my husband and I decided to wait to tell Pamela. In addition to being a straight A sophomore student, she was in the middle of a winning basketball season where she was the team's star point guard. Pamela was experiencing a wonderful year—things couldn't be better for this beautiful, well-adjusted fifteen-year-old. How do I give her news that will rob her of all of her contentment and place her on a path of uncertainty? We decided to wait until after the holiday season.

The waiting was hard. We tried not to alter our behavior so as not to make her suspicious in any way. I had to resist hugging her too much. I had to resist the urge to call her a million times during the day just to hear her voice. I had to resist the urge to say *I love you* more than the normal times a day. It was hard not telling her. It was especially hard once we started talking to doctors and other family members. While we wanted to get her through the holidays, we did not want her to be the last to know. And so we waited and we prayed and we asked God to direct us to the right time to tell Pamela.

The holiday season was quiet and warm and passed quickly. About a week after Christmas, just before the final games of the District Basketball tournament, my husband and I knew that we had to tell Pamela that I had cancer. My husband felt that it would be best if she heard it directly from me. And I decided that the best approach would be to tell her as directly as possible. *Pamela, I have cancer . . .* This was the hardest thing I have ever had to do. I watched her intently as I told her the news. She was so brave, but my mother's eye didn't miss the tears that welled up in her eyes. I didn't miss the brief look of panic or the tremble of her lips. I missed nothing and I wished with all my heart that I could take the words back or at least say that they didn't mean anything. I wished that I could give that mother's assurance that I would give when she was two, *it's going to be alright*. But I couldn't. All my husband and I could offer our daughter was what we had tried to give her as a child—our faith. We talked to her about God's power and God's love. We shared our faith in a God who is a healer and who will walk with us through this battle with cancer. We offered to answer her questions and to not keep anything from her from this point on. We prayed with her and we held her tight and we let her know that love is forever. As I watched her walk away, I knew that life for her would never be the same, but I rested in the confidence of knowing that God has her and God will take care of her.

Dear Lord, give us your strength as we share this news with those we love. Bless our children, our spouses, our siblings, our parents, and our friends. Lord, give us the words to say. Take care of them and help them to trust you to take care of us. May our faith encourage them to live for you. Amen.

Don't Pity Me

THE WORD CANCER INVOKES PITY. News of my illness spread rapidly. Once my church family was made aware, I was placed on prayer lists all over the city and the country. And once my hair fell out, it was apparent to many that what they had heard was indeed true. But instead of support, from many it solicited pity. When people pity you, their voice tone changes. There is a certain look in their eyes when they look at you. They find it hard to look you directly in the eyes. They touch you and they speak condescending words. Their lips drip of soothing words to take all of the reality out of your ordeal. *It's going to be alright . . . you look sooo good . . . you keep hanging in there*. Stop, look at me. I'm sick, not dead, and I don't want your pity.

For me, people's pity sounded like a death sentence. I felt that they had given up on me. I felt that they were more concerned about helping me die than they were about helping me to live. I don't need to be talked to like I'm a child. Talk to me about the things we used to talk about. Talk to me as the same person I was before cancer walked into my life. Talk to me about your faith and your testimony of faith. Ask me how I feel; don't assume that you know how I feel. Ask me the questions that are behind your false smile. Ask me if they've said I'm going to die; don't assume that they have. TALK TO ME—don't pity me.

Before I was diagnosed with cancer, I had never encountered pity before. I didn't know what it looked like or how it felt. The first time I encountered it as a cancer patient, it shook me—it stunned me. I saw an old friend who had obviously heard the news of my illness and as she greeted me, I was shocked. *She pities me!* I couldn't believe what I saw because I did not think of myself as one to be pitied. But the pity I saw in her eyes caused me to back up and think, *maybe I'm being too casual with this thing. Is there something I don't understand? Should I pity myself?* All of these thoughts ran through my mind. And then I remembered who I was and what I knew about the God I serve. And I looked into my sister's eyes and I smiled. I demanded pity to take a back seat. I began to affirm in her that pity has no place in our relationship or in our conversation today. And I began to share that God is gracious—whether we are sick or well.

Pity has a way of overshadowing God's grace. And during this journey I have decided that I will not allow pity to do that. So don't pity me—not with cancer or without it. Pity is the enemy of faith. And I'm walking by faith. I want to be a testimony to others that God is a healer.

Dear Lord, we give you thanks for another day. We realize how awesome your grace is in our lives. Lord, help us to ward off the effects of pity that can often cause us to doubt your healing power in our lives. Lord, we thank you for the love and compassion of others. Help us to speak words of affirmation that will strengthen their faith. Amen.

Life Goes On

YOU HAVE CANCER, BUT LIFE GOES ON. When you first get diagnosed with cancer, life literally stops. For about a week, things are different. You think and act differently. You seem to even look differently. Your family treats you differently—more tenderly, with kid gloves. But you soon discover that life goes on. You cannot, nor will God allow you to, live in this sheltered world called cancer. *Get up and go back to living.* Things are different, but in a real sense they are the same. Work has to get done, the household routine has to go on, schedules have to be kept, and relationships have to be maintained. You cannot get on a mountaintop and declare, *I have cancer. Life, I need you to take a pause.*

Life goes on. This does not mean that no one cares about you but it means that we have to live regardless of our disease. I must admit, I needed a moment to pause and to think about what having cancer meant in the routine scheme of things. I toyed with taking a few days off to go off by myself to clear my head and to think through this cancer thing. But being a woman with responsibilities, I could never find the time. I didn't seem to have the luxury of escaping life for even a brief moment. Life had to go on. There were people in my life who didn't know about my struggle and they were waiting for me to show up. There were responsibilities that had to be met regardless of my illness. Life had to go on—with or without me.

I discovered that while God has placed me here on earth with a distinct purpose in mind, life can go on without me. I discovered that it's not about whether or not I am indispensable, it's about doing what we can while we can. I learned that God called us to remain present in this thing called life for as long as we are able. Each new day calls the roll and if God allows us to see it, God expects us to answer, *Present*. The blessing of each new day is another opportunity to be a blessing to someone else.

There were times when I wanted to take a long pause. Often I wanted to take to my bed, skip certain things, pull back, back up, just lay down. But God would not allow it to be so. Life would not allow it to be so. There was always something that claimed my attention and my energy and my time. There was always something that I needed to complete or to be involved in. At first, I thought it was too much and maybe I needed to slow down. But I soon realized that it was simply life calling to me, *Pat, get back in the game, life goes on!* I realized that it was a loving God calling me to be present and attentive, God calling to me in my shell of isolation from the world and coaxing me out and back into a life full of living. It was God pushing me and pulling me back into a life worth living. And, yes, it was God reminding me that I would be met every day by God's abundant grace.

Dear Lord, thank you for reminding us to live life to its fullest. Thank you for not allowing us to hide in the midst of our pain and frustration. Lord, we need you to help us face each new day. May your love and care be fresh and abundant with each new day. Amen.

You're So Strong

YOU'RE SO STRONG! If I hear that one more time, I think I'll scream. If one more person says that to me, I'll lose it. How do you know how strong I am? Do you think I'm strong because I came out of the house today? Do you think I'm strong because I didn't stay at home in the bed today? Do you think I'm strong because I've decided to live life today and not give up? What does it mean when you say to me *you're so strong?* I didn't get up today to be a martyr. I got up because I have to—I have to push forward; I can't give up.

I wish I could see what others see. I don't see the strength they talk about. And I don't want to be set up. I still cry at night when everyone else is asleep. I still fall apart some mornings when I look in the mirror. There are some days when panic sets in and I feel as if I can't make it. I am not a hero. I am not strong. I am no stronger than anyone else who has to face life with all of its uncertainties and its pain and its tribulations. And when you spend such enormous amounts of time telling me how strong I am, I feel that I have to live up to this unattainable set of expectations. What if I feel like crying? What if you catch me on one of my "bad" days? What if I fail you? What if I don't provide the modeling that you need to keep your faith strong?

Strength is so relative. It depends on what you have experienced in your own life or what you have come to expect from strong people. Whatever people saw or did not see in me was the result of what I had lived with all of my life. I had seen parents who struggled with serious illnesses all of their lives. I had seen them deal with their illnesses in ways that kept the family intact and provided lessons in strength for me and my brother. What I did was model what I had seen my father do when he worked in the midst of great pain. I modeled what I saw my mother do when she kept the family together in spite of my father's illness. The silent message was that you never give up. I soon realized that what people were seeing was the strength and faith of my parents.

During times of illness, we draw on the strength of those who have gone on before us. Their model of strength becomes our source of strength. The God of our ancestors rises up in us too. The legacy of strength that belongs to us as women comes through at those times when we most need it. I come from a long line of strong black women who have endured all kinds of hardships. And their spirits hold me and lift me and rise up in me during my illness. The blessing of God's grace is the power that has already been released in our mothers and our grandmothers and our sisters and our girlfriends. And that power has been passed on to us that, as women, our strength might be a testimony and a source of strength to others.

Dear Lord, thank you for making us strong. As women, often we are thought of as frail and weak but your power in us gives us the strength to face every obstacle. Thank you for standing up in us and allowing others to see your power. We are so grateful to you for your awesome strength in our lives. Amen.

Where Can I Hide?

I JUST WANT TO HIDE. It seems that everyone knows that I'm sick. Everywhere I go, everyone wants to know how I'm doing. All I do is tell the story over and over and answer question after question. I really don't want to see anyone else. I want to hide. I want to go where no one knows me and no one knows that I have cancer.

I used to hear about people taking to their beds when they had to face trouble in their lives. I wish I could do the same but for me it doesn't seem to be an option. Even though I have to be in the stream of things and life goes on, there are days when I wish I could hide. I wish for some time with myself, away from the questions and the stares and, yes, away from the cancer. I want to hide in a place that is pre-cancer—a place where my concern is for the trivial things of life like what movie I will watch tonight on TV or what color lipstick I will wear that will match my dress. I wish I could return to that carefree time when everything was not seen through the eyes of my sickness.

Even if I could hide, what am I hiding from? That's a good question. On those days when I get out of bed and I feel the need to hide, I have to confront myself with the question: *Pat, what do you want to hide from?* Sometimes I just want to hide from the roles I have to play. I want to hide from that person that everyone looks up to for strength and for comfort. Sometimes I want to hide from the stares and the questions that I don't feel like answering. Sometimes I want to hide from the good intentions of others. I want to have my life back where others are not so concerned about caring for me. Sometimes I just want to hide from a life that seems to be going on without me. Let me sit for a while and collect my thoughts and watch from a distance and then get back in the swing of things. Let me hide for a minute.

I remember when I was a child and we would play *hide-and-seek*. The goal was to find a good spot for hiding so that no one could find you. And when you found that spot it was so exciting to watch people come looking for you and not find you. Often you could see them, but they could not see you. They would be so close but still miss your hiding spot. Sometimes you would have to cover your mouth to keep from giggling at the fact that they were so close but still not able to find you. But I distinctly remember that the game lost its excitement if they gave up and stopped looking for you. You would run out and declare, *Here I am!* Maybe that's my dilemma. I want to hide but I don't want the people whom I love and care for to ever stop looking for me.

The good news is that God refuses to let me stay in hiding. Some days I try; I have some good hiding places—my office, my bedroom. But God keeps looking for me—invades my hiding space—sends family and loved ones into my space. And I'm glad to be found because after a while it gets lonely in my hiding place and I realize that I need the smile, kind word, and embrace of others. So I come out and I accept the love that they so freely offer, and I thank God that God has not left me alone but has sent grace and mercy to be my constant companions.

Dear Lord, today was one of our "feel like hiding" days. But we thank you for reminding us that we can never be without your presence and your love. Thank you for coaxing us out of hiding time and time again. Help us to live from day to day knowing that we are never alone. Amen.

I'm Tired

I'M TIRED. I can't say that out loud to anyone, but when I think about the journey that lies ahead I'm tired already. I want this journey to be over and it is just beginning. I'm tired of the treatment and the appointments and the medicine. I'm tired of being sick and I'm tired of being tired. And I can't say it out loud to anyone. When I go for each appointment, I smile and patiently answer their questions and try hard not to complain. But I want to scream, *I'm tired!*

I've always kept an awesome activity pace. I never stayed still long enough to be tired. Oh, I know what it is to feel tired after some of those sixty-hour weeks and twelve-hour days. But to be tired for no apparent reason—to wake up tired—is new for me. I find it hard to deal with living with tiredness, to have no energy after doing one thing when I used to do five things at once and be energized doing it. I still find myself shocked at how easily I get tired. And the tiredness is not just physical; it's mental and emotional as well. Sometimes the stress of doing just one thing drives me to tears. Sometimes I can't think clearly or as quickly as I want to. This causes me great frustration. I get up late and I go to bed early because I'm just tired. I can't stay up to be with my husband or talk to my daughter because I'm tired. And I can't really remember if this was how I was before or if it's a result of my illness. But what I know for sure is that being tired is a way of life and I'm tired of being tired.

Being tired is no fun. It makes life dull and boring. I want to do things, but after a few minutes I get tired. I'm too tired to read; too tired to exercise; too tired to go out of the house; too tired to talk; too tired to do little more than watch TV in between naps. I often find myself spending hours in the bedroom sleeping. But the surprising thing is that I get these amazing bursts of energy that keep me up writing or working on a project or praying about the church. And when I'm working on these things, I don't get tired—I seem to gain some new resource of strength. But as soon as I finish, I'm dead tired.

The worst kind of tiredness for me is the emotional tiredness that I sometimes feel. This cancer thing sometimes makes me tired emotionally—I feel like giving up. I feel like just lying around and doing nothing. And I'm not sure how to handle that. But what God is showing me is that it's alright to do nothing sometimes. God has released me to lie in bed some mornings and some afternoons. God has surprised me with those small, strong bursts of energy that let me know that I have an energy source that is beyond me. I am so grateful for the days when I look back and see how much God allowed me to accomplish. I am ecstatic to see how much I have been able to continue to do in spite of being tired, and I know it is because of the power of a loving God who pushes me past my human limit and allows me to operate by God's grace. For this I am truly grateful.

Dear Lord, thank you for today! Thank you that today we were able to get up and move through our schedule with a reasonable portion of strength. You keep us alive and vibrant in spite of our sickness. Bless us and keep the tiredness away. Amen.

You Look Beautiful

YOU LOOK BEAUTIFUL. Many people tell me that. They say I don't look as if I have cancer. Even with my hair gone, they say I look beautiful. But often when I look in the mirror, I don't see beautiful. I see the blotches in my skin. I see the discoloration. I see the peeling skin and rough skin. I see the hair gone all over my body. And many days I don't feel beautiful. But I have to listen to what people say and they say I'm beautiful.

This journey has certainly caused me to assess what beauty really is. As a woman, we spend most of our lives trying to look good—we want to be beautiful. But cancer makes you look at yourself in ways that you've never looked before. You notice everything. It's amazing how we look in the mirror at ourselves at least once every day and we miss so much. But cancer will not allow you to miss anything. You notice the slightest change in your appearance—the slightest discoloration, the tiniest pimple, the smallest weight gain. Everything is significant and profound. And it becomes so important that we look good.

I've had to wrestle with my appearance. I find myself paying much more attention to how I look now than I did before I was diagnosed with cancer. I find myself being much more intentional about what I wear and how it fits and how the colors coordinate. I want to look good, not like someone who is sick. And as I have struggled with how I look, I have discovered the beauty that lies with. I have owned my beauty in a way that I didn't before. And because I am comfortable, I have been able to define what cancer looks like in ways that destroy the concepts that many people have.

I dress to suit me and no one else. I have discovered that it's not about what others think but it's about what makes me feel beautiful on any given day. So some days I wrap my head, on other days I wear hats, and on most days I let my bald head show. I have discovered that there is no right way to look beautiful; the choice is mine to make. And I have made it and I have discovered that beauty is a state of mind, and beauty comes from the heart of God. Beauty starts with that inner peace that only God can give. Beauty is when the love of God overflows into your inner being and you see yourself as God sees you. And when you look at that person through the eyes of God, you see a beautiful person smiling back.

You look beautiful. Now when someone says that to me, I simply smile and say thank you because I realize that it's not sympathy but it's a gift from God. I realize that once again God has sent me a reminder that the beauty of who I am cannot be destroyed by anything—not even cancer.

Dear Lord, thank you for making me beautiful. Thank you for reminding us as women that our real beauty rests in you. Thank you, God, for the wonderful angels that you send our way to speak words of compliment that make us feel good as women. As we walk in our beauty, we will give honor and glory to your name. Amen.

I Don't Feel Like Praying

I DON'T FEEL LIKE PRAYING! You would think that during a time like this, that's all I would want to do. But strangely enough, I found there were times—no, *periods*—when I didn't feel like praying. There were times when I couldn't pray—simply didn't want to pray. Those times were strange and I felt so disconnected from God. But I could not make myself pray. I would pick up my meditation books, read a few lines, and put them down. I would start a prayer, only to drift off into sleep.

What was so amazing is that while I didn't feel like praying, people were praying for me constantly. Everywhere I went, people were reminding me: *I'm praying for you*. I couldn't tell them I didn't feel like praying. I could pray in public. I could pray for others. But my private prayer life was almost non-existent. What in the world is wrong with me? It caused me to doubt my faith and doubt my relationship with God. Why can't I pray? Why am I not able to talk to God? Am I angry with God? What is it?

I never got an answer. So I decided to just live with not being able to pray. Strangely, I never felt that God was not with me. I felt disconnected, to be sure, but protected and loved at the same time. I decided to rely on the relationship I had with God—that regardless, God would love and care for me. I allowed my prayer life to be what it was—not to struggle with it but to accept it for what it was. I didn't feel I could talk to anyone about what I was going through, so I didn't. I just silently placed myself and my prayer life in the hands of a God whom I trusted to work it out. I believed that my relationship with God was so deep that it transcended even my ability to pray.

In my period of not praying consistently, I learned a lot about God and God's grace. I learned once again that it's not about us, it's about God. It's about a God who is able to love us in spite of us. It's about a God who can communicate with us even when we can't or won't pray. It's about a God who will not allow the lines of communication to be permanently shut down. It's about a God who will eventually say enough is enough and gently call us back to prayer. I learned to be still and to trust God.

Prayer is a wonderful gift from God. Prayer is a wonderful avenue of communication with God. I praise God that eventually and slowly, my prayer life returned. And not only did it return, it was stronger than ever. I value my ability to pray but I realize that my relationship with God goes even beyond my ability to pray. God does understand our hearts. God understands hearts that are struggling. God understands that we often struggle with being sick and the possibility of never being well. God understands and is patient to bring us back to him in prayer. I thank God for his patience and his covering grace. I thank God for not allowing me to stay out of touch too long. I thank God for never leaving nor forsaking me.

Dear Lord, thank you for your constant and abiding love. Lord, give us the desire to pray, the desire to talk to you each day. Lord, help us to stay in touch with you, in spite of our pain and frustration. Lord, we know you love us and we truly want to serve you more. Please continue to draw us close to you. Speak to our hearts day by day. Amen.

When Panic Sets In

PANIC IS ONE OF THOSE ELUSIVE EMOTIONS. It's quick; it comes on you fast, often before you can prepare yourself for its coming. And just as you're getting ready to deal with it, it's gone. Panic can cause panic because it keeps you off balance—sometimes panic makes you think that you're losing your mind. *Did I really feel that? What's going on?*

There came a time when I had to deal with panic—panic attacks, feelings of panic that left me exhausted and fearful. I had always prided myself with being able to handle things. I was never the type of person who easily fell apart when things first happened. I would have my moment later after the event, in private where I could think things through and pray my way out. But with my cancer came panic—deep panic—the kind of panic that at times took root.

Panic came at times when I didn't expect it. Panic came at times when there was no reason to panic. Panic came when the doctor's visit yielded a good report and on days when I felt good and during times when things seemed to be looking up. I would be in the midst of enjoying the good things and panic would jump on me and leave me trembling, or shake me awake and leave me sleepless for the rest of the night, or drive me to tears for no apparent reason. Panic was sometimes constant and always troubling.

You have to fight your way through panic. Panic can and will become a constant companion unless it is dealt with. I was driven to that point after experiencing a horrible panic attack while having lunch with a friend. In the middle of a very pleasant lunch at one of my favorite restaurants, I found myself unable to breathe. My friend was talking and I was looking at her and nodding—but I could not breathe. I felt as if I was dying but I couldn't say anything. I was horrified. She eventually saw what she later described as the "terror" in my eyes and asked me what was wrong. All I could say was that I needed to go home because I didn't feel well. The panic had consumed me and taken full control. I remember getting in my car and once I left the restaurant, driving into a shopping mall parking lot where I cried and asked God to help me.

I remember God's warm comfort on that troubling day. Although I was still quite shaken, I felt that my prayers had been answered. I learned to give myself the room to be real about what was happening to my body. I learned to allow the feelings inside me to go full circle. I learned that God was with me and holding me and breathing for me when my situation literally took my breath away. During those times I heard God saying, *Breathe, breathe, Pat,* and I am able to take the next breath and continue my journey forward.

Dear Lord, please be our source of strength when we're afraid. Help us to not be in fear but to trust you in all things. Be our breath during those times when we feel anxious and cannot breathe for ourselves. Drive the panic away from your children this day and give us your divine peace. Amen.

Do I Want to Live?

DO I WANT TO LIVE? This question came out of nowhere one day as I returned from a chemo session that was particularly draining. The schedule was getting to me; it was draining me. Every moment was filled by the things that my cancer had placed on the calendar. There was no time to really live. Every day was filled with either being too sick to do anything or going to a doctor's appointment. When I did feel like doing something, it drained me and it took days to get back to normal. I had to ask myself, do I really want to live like this? Do I think I can live like this? Is this really living?

I had heard that many people chose not to take the treatments because they were too painful and draining. In fact I had watched one of my favorite professors at the seminary take such a route. When his cancer came back for the second time, he met with his family and told them he had decided to allow the disease to take its course without any treatment. In the months prior to his death, he appeared to be at peace. When I preached in chapel, his final encouraging words to me were: *Thank you, Pat, for that sermon.*

But every decision is personal and just as quickly as the question was raised in my spirit, it was dismissed. The answer was not as profound as the question. Gently, the reassurance of God moved me to accept the fact that I was supposed to live. The days were still painful and full of uncertainty, but the spirit of God became a daily source of comfort and began to pour back into my desire to live and not die. I remember when the Lord led me to read Psalm 118 and spoke to my heart that I had to live to be a testimony of God's power to heal and to restore.

My preaching during my illness was therapeutic. The word was received by me first, and then I had to share it with those who, like me, often felt like giving up. When I preached *I Will Not Die but Live*, the Spirit of God moved in a marvelous way to bring healing to everyone present and to encourage us all to not give up but to allow God to speak life to our souls. *Do I want to live? Yes, I do.* God is not finished with me yet, and I yield to his divine will for my life.

Dear Lord, thank you for comforting us when we feel like giving up. Thank you for reminding us that even our very lives belong to you. Thank you for reminding us that by your power we do not have to die; we can live. Give us the desire to live according to your will for our lives. Amen.

On a Scale from 1–10

WHAT'S YOUR PAIN ON A SCALE FROM 1–10? This was the question that everyone asked—every nurse, every technician, every doctor. Pain was their reference point for dealing with me. Before they talked to me, before they examined me, they asked, *What's your level of pain from 1–10?* This question defines how you feel about yourself. It reminds you that pain is the norm; pain is inevitable; pain is who you are to other people. There is no possibility of there not being pain.

I can always remember seeing the pain chart in examination rooms, but before I was diagnosed with cancer the chart didn't mean a lot to me. I remember thinking that the chart was a little too simple; why not simply ask people how they feel? But now I look at the pain chart differently. Now that pain is a constant companion, the pain chart claims my attention when I enter the room. Now I can't ignore the chart that ranges from the happy, smiling face representing #0 to the crying face that represents #10. Now I have to deal with how I feel, and in doing so I have come to realize that sometimes I can't express in words how I feel. Now I appreciate the faces associated with the levels of pain. I've been all over the chart—from 1–10.

I can remember my range of feelings in dealing with what I began to refer to as the "pain question." *What's your pain on a scale from 1-10?* Some days I was between numbers, *somewhere between four and five.* Some days I was definitive—*it's a six.* Some days the question reduced me to tears or the question gave me great joy because it was a "good day" when my pain was not so severe. The question always led to more conversation about where and what kind of pain it was and how long I had felt that way. I often found myself thinking, *is there anything else we can talk about other than my pain?*

But I learned to thank God for the question because the question allowed me to see the awesome power of God to deal with our pain and to move us beyond our pain in the healing journey. One day my pain was pretty high. While I waited for the nurse, anticipating the question and getting my answer ready, I was reminded of the pains of this life. I was reminded that every day we are confronted with the question: *what's your pain on a scale of 1-10?* Every day, we have to deal with the mental, emotional, and spiritual pain that robs us of our joy and peace. Every day God asks: *what's your pain on a scale from 1-10?* And like in the examination room, God meets us at the point of our pain and comforts us. Every day, I get to give this pain to the One who has the power to remove it or to give me the strength to endure it.

Dear Lord, please minister to all of those in pain today. Release our bodies from the pain associated with this disease and give us physical relief. Heal our emotional and spiritual pain. Give us what we stand in need of to endure. Amen.

Can I Trust My Doctor?

MY DOCTOR IS CONSIDERED ONE OF THE BEST IN THE WORLD WHEN IT COMES TO CANCER TREATMENT. When I was diagnosed with stage-3 cancer, I was pleased to have him as my doctor, as I felt that he would be very aggressive in his treatment.

But as the disease progressed and after my treatment started, I found myself asking: *Can I trust my doctor?* The question didn't originate with regard to his competence or even his bedside manner; it had to do with my being reassured that we shared the same desire for my complete healing. I needed to know that he believed that I could and I would be healed. I didn't just want to be another patient. I wanted to feel special and to feel that he would do for me what he would do for his own mother, wife, or sister. I wanted to be able to trust him with my life. I wasn't sure that I could.

I have always stressed to our congregation to make it a point to know the faith position of anyone and everyone who services you in any way. Know whether your beautician, nail technician, cleaners, mechanic, etc. share your faith beliefs. But for saying that and living by that prior to my cancer diagnosis, I had no clue about my doctor. Everything I heard about my doctor was positive and he was certainly pleasant enough. But still my spirit was not at rest.

On my pre-surgery visit, my doctor was extremely patient and thorough in explaining everything that would happen and what I could expect post-surgery. My husband and I listened intently and my husband, who is always thorough, began to ask the questions that we had discussed between ourselves. All of them were answered to our satisfaction. But then the doctor asked: *Do you have any more questions?* And it was at that moment that I knew what I needed to know. So I asked, *Do you know Him?* The doctor was confused: *Know who?* Me: *Do you know God?* I remember the room getting silent. The nurse didn't know what to say, and my doctor folded his clipboard over his chest and leaned back against the wall and said, *Yes, I'm a Presbyterian and I go to church.* At this my husband sat down in preparation for what he knew I was going to say next. By the power of God, I was able to say to my doctor, *You're going to operate on my body and I need to know not that you go to church but that you know Him because you're going to need to know Him and believe in Him.* And as he turned slightly red in the face, he said with a great deal of sincerity, *No one has ever asked me that, but Yes, I do know Him and I do rely on Him whenever I go into the operating room. Thank you for reminding me of that.* That's all I needed to know. And once that was said, I was able to trust him and to feel much more comfortable about the surgery. I have a great doctor and I think God used me to allow him to realize his Source.

My faith is important to me and I need to know that it's important to those whom I meet along this journey. I thank God every day for a doctor who knows the Lord. I continue to lift him up that whenever he does surgery he might be God's instrument of healing.

Dear Lord, bless all of the doctors, nurses, and caregivers who have been called to minister to others. Give them your divine wisdom and skill. May they love and serve you always. Amen.

But This Is My Body

ONE OF MY FIRST PURCHASES WAS *THE BREAST BOOK*. It was recommended by my doctor and was the size of four books put together. I read this book constantly, probably more than the Bible. Every word that the doctor said sent me to *The Breast Book*. I used it as a reference book to help me understand everything that was said about my condition. I would stay up late, reading, underlining, and highlighting. But one day, I decided to put the book down because in spite of what the book said, I realized that my body was different. I realized that no matter what the "book" said and what the "book" suggested, in the final analysis, *this is my body!*

It takes a while to fully understand in our heart what we know in our head: we only get one body and we have to take care of it. This is especially true of women, especially sick women. We rely on others to tell us what we should do with our most prized possession, our bodies. I can't count the numerous decisions that have been made by others with regard to my health. But it was during my illness that I finally dared to take full control of my body and that I dared to make the decisions that made me feel good about me.

I remember the first discussion I had with the doctor about the surgery that he felt would save my life. It was determined that in order to save my life, I would need to have a mastectomy. I remember the doctor suggesting that I would want to have the reconstruction done at the same time or as soon as possible afterward. I decided that I did not want reconstruction. Immediately, I felt the disapproval of my doctor: Of course I would want reconstruction, why would I want to live disfigured when I could have reconstruction done? I remember saying to him, *But it's my body.*

Yes, during this process, I had to claim my body as my own. I had to remind doctors and nurses and other well-meaning friends that I would not relinquish control of my body to anyone. Surprisingly, my husband, who generally was highly opinionated and an in-charge person, stood solidly with me in my decision to control every decision with regard to my body. He fought with doctors, nurses, and family members to make sure that they did not forget my wishes or negate my concerns and dismiss my choices. He fully supported my decision to claim full ownership of the body God has loaned me. In this process, God reminded me of my stewardship responsibility—to present my body as a sacrifice to God's glory and honor. And how I presented that body—*my body*—was my decision, my choice.

Dear Lord, help us to remember that our body belongs to you. During this journey, give us the courage to make decisions and choices that are in line with your perfect will for us, not on what others desire for us. Lord, thank you for this beautiful body that you have clothed us in. May all of the decisions we make with regard to it bring glory and honor to you. Amen.

Letting Go

"YOU KNOW YOU WILL NOT BE ABLE TO KEEP UP THE SCHEDULE YOU PRESENTLY HAVE." As I listened to the doctor gently caution me, I was way ahead of him. My body had already given me notice that it would be impossible to do what I had been doing if I had any desire to survive. But knowing that fact and being able to let go of all the things I was juggling was another thing. I was the one who had shared with my students and church members the art of juggling: *keep your eye on one ball at a time*. Not only did I tell the story, I lived it. I was used to moving from one thing to another with relative ease, constantly juggling all of the roles in my life: wife, mother, daughter, professor, pastor, and friend. I had mastered the art of juggling but now as I became sicker and sicker, everything was in danger of crashing to the floor. I knew it was time for letting go, not just some things but everything.

Letting go is hard when you're used to doing a lot. It's hard to give up everything when you're used to doing everything. I eventually became so sick that I had to let go of most of the things I was used to doing. There were some things that I considered not an option. I chose to continue being a pastor to the more than 200 people called Faith Community Baptist Church. I even continued to work with a small group of women in the public housing projects near our church. But I knew that just about everything else would have to go. I would have to stop teaching at the seminary and give up all of my sorority participation. My husband went with me to inform my Dean that I would have to take a leave from my teaching duties at the seminary. I still remember the love and concern and encouragement that was given as the Dean rearranged the schedule to allow me to take a sabbatical for two semesters. But it was hard and I shed tears as I thought about the students who I would not be able to see through to graduation. Letting go was hard!

I gave up all household duties: cooking, washing, cleaning. Most of those were taken on by my husband with the help of family and friends. I was told that my only job was to get well. So I got used to not working 12-hour days and not going from one meeting to the next. I got used to not multi-tasking as I did the job of wife, mother, pastor, and professor. I had to get used to being at home—all day—with nothing to do. I never realized how much of my time was devoted to doing—there was rarely a time when I was not doing something. It was only when I didn't have the energy that I began to realize how much energy went into living from day to day.

Letting go was hard! But in letting go, I discovered the true meaning of that familiar saying *Let go and let God.* For it was in letting go that I was able to spend more quality time with God—time that was not hindered by my busyness. I discovered the peace and gentleness of being quiet and sitting in silence and hearing my own heartbeat and allowing myself time to breathe. I discovered that I enjoyed my own company. Letting go was hard but letting go blessed me and allowed me to receive God's presence in many marvelous ways. It was in the letting go that I was finally able to allow God to heal me.

Dear Lord, give us the strength to let go of all those things that we feel we must keep doing. Help us to give these things to you and to allow you to heal our bodies. Lord, help us to know that we are much more than what we do. Help us to let go and let you heal us! Amen.

Possibility
FAITH

*Then [Jesus] said to her,
"Daughter, your faith has healed you. Go in peace."*
LUKE 8:48, NIV

*Hearing this, Jesus said to Jairus,
"Don't be afraid; just believe, and she will be healed."*
LUKE 8:50, NIV

Our text for today is about healing. Jesus heals a woman who has been bleeding for twelve years, and Jesus heals Jairus's daughter. Jesus heals because Jesus is a healer. These are marvelous stories—stories that stir our faith and cause us to shout with joy. These stories help us remain faithful in the midst of life's hard situations. This is the kind of story that we need as we make our way through this "cancer" journey.

If the truth be told, our faith is at its strongest when things are working out—when things are going well—when Jesus is responding how we want him to and when we want him to. It's in those moments when it's less obvious and less dramatic that we have some concerns. What do we do when he does not come when we want him to and when he is not on time? In our text Jairus leaves home with a daughter who is dying. A woman who has been bleeding for twelve years confronts Jesus although many doctors have not been able to help her. Their situations appear to be impossible. It appears to be too late. It appears as if there is nothing that the Lord can do. But they both seem to press beyond what appears to be possible to exercise Possibility Faith.

Possibility Faith is a faith that says there might be a *possibility* that something can be done. Have you ever been there? All of us have—daily we are confronted by life's impossibilities. All of us have dealt with exercising Possibility Faith. When we're confronted with the doctor's final prognosis—when the lawyer gives his final conclusion—and it appears to be final—we have to operate on Possibility Faith. We have to pray and trust before we see—before God answers. We have to put it in the hands of the God who makes ALL things possible and who is WELL-ABLE to do whatever we need done.

Jairus is a synagogue leader. He is a person of authority in Jewish society. He is used to people attending to his every need. He is used to people coming to him for what they needed. But Jairus's twelve-year-old daughter is dying and he has heard that there is an itinerant preacher in town who has the ability to heal. Jesus presents the possibility that his daughter might be healed. Jairus practices Possibility Faith by daring to ask. Jairus is a leader but he is willing to humble himself and ask Jesus for what he needs and what he wants. Jairus does what was probably shocking to those around him—he falls at Jesus' feet and he begs Jesus repeatedly: *My little girl is dying. Please come home with me and lay hands on her so she can be healed.*

Based on what he has heard about Jesus, Jairus is willing to ask. Jairus is willing to ask because he sees the possibility of healing for his daughter. How many times have we failed to ask? How many times have we suffered unnecessarily because we failed to ask the Lord for what we needed and what we wanted? Asking is an act of faith. Asking is the greatest act of faith we can express. To ask the Lord is to declare that we believe there's a possibility for our prayers to be answered. *Closed mouths don't get fed.*

Somebody needs to ask God today. Whatever it is that you're seeking—ask the Lord today. Humble yourself and get down on your knees and beg the Lord to do what you need him to do. Love will make you ask—need will make you ask—Possibility Faith is the faith to ask. The songwriter declares: *Ask what you will of the Savior and it shall not be in vain. Call when you need his assistance, he will hear when you call his name!*

JUST ASK!

Immediately after Jairus dares to ask Jesus to come and heal his daughter, Jesus is confronted by a woman who has been bleeding for twelve years. She is in a pitiful state: her bleeding makes her ceremonially unclean and unfit to go in public. She is poor—she has spent all of her money going from doctor to doctor, none of whom could heal her. But this woman dares to exercise Possibility Faith because she has heard that there is a possibility that Jesus can heal her after all these years. She makes a bold move: she comes out in public defying the religious mores of her day; she gets in the middle of the crowd and inches her way close to Jesus, and when no one can stop her she reaches out and touches the fringes of his ceremonial stole that is hanging down his back. She reaches out. Possibility Faith dares to reach out.

Her reaching out is not without risk. She could have been permanently put out of the city. She could have been disciplined by the church for touching a holy man while she was bleeding. She could have been forever declared an outcast. But she was willing to risk it all for the possibility of being healed.

Possibility Faith is taking the risk to do what you have never done before. Possibility Faith requires that we reach out—that we move beyond our comfort zone—that we do what may appear to be crazy, inappropriate, unnecessary, and uncomfortable. Possibility Faith will drive you to reach out to the Lord—to reach out in ways that you have never reached out to him before. Possibility Faith will cause you to pray like you have never prayed before. Possibility Faith will cause you to pray at times and in places that you have never prayed before. Possibility Faith will cause you to reach out to the Lord every day, all day—your mind, heart, and soul will seek the Lord in ways that will be new, refreshing, and wonderful. Reach out—the Lord is available to you. Reach out—the Lord is waiting for you to reach out. Reach out and experience his healing power in your life!

This text is about healing. Both the twelve-year-old girl and the woman with an issue of blood for twelve years are healed. The father and the woman have the faith to ask and the faith to reach out AND they also have the faith to believe. The faith to believe is always our challenge. In the text, Jairus's daughter dies while Jairus and Jesus are on the way to the house. And Jairus's friends encourage him to stop bothering Jesus because she has died and it appears as if there is nothing else that can be done. BUT Jesus encourages Jairus by saying, *Do not fear; only believe.* It's easy to believe when things are going right—when we can see some improvement—when it appears as if it might work out. But belief is a challenge when we don't know what's going to happen. Belief is challenging when healing is less obvious, less dramatic, and seemingly less miraculous. What do you do when you don't know what God will do? We have to believe.

Our belief is ALL we have. We don't have any other choice BUT to believe in the power and grace of Almighty God. When my brother was in the hospital and we listened as the doctor told us that essentially there was nothing more they could do, I remember grasping his hands and looking into his eyes and saying, *I know what the doctors are saying, but we're just going to pray and see what God will do.*

God heals in our text, but sometimes healing does not occur in the way we desire it to occur. But we have to practice Possibility Faith. We can never stop believing and trusting God to heal and to do the impossible. My brother died believing that God was a healer—and God did answer our prayers for healing in him on the other side. And what God had to show me is that on April 11, 2012, there were some people that were healed—on this side. The good news of today is that we can never give up—we can never stop asking—we can never stop reaching out—we can never stop believing, because God is still God and God is still willing to meet us at the point of our every need.

Today, God is calling us to not let go of our faith. In the midst of whatever we're up against, let us keep walking by faith and not by sight. God is calling us to keep the faith, even when we can't see our way out. Keep the faith because this is the faith that keeps us going from day to day. This is the faith that keeps hope alive. This is the faith that keep us living in the midst of all we have to face. This is Possibility Faith: the possibility that God will answer—the possibility that God will heal—the possibility that God might change things—the possibility that God might perform a miracle—the possibility that God will heal because God has done it for others—because God has done it before—because God is a loving God and a kind God.

So whatever we go through, keep the faith—keep on calling his name—keep on clinging to him—keep on holding on to God's unchanging hand. Keep on serving a God who is able to turn the impossible things of this life into possibility.

A Surgery Date

FINALLY, I HAVE A SURGERY DATE. Through the weeks of chemo, I have longed for a surgery date. It seems as if not having a surgery date adds to the uncertainty of my illness. Having no surgery date adds to the frustration and seems to keep things up in the air. I have waited for a surgery date. I have been impatient for a surgery date. I have asked repeatedly about a surgery date. So finally I have a surgery date: August 1st.

It's amazing what a surgery date does to the spirit. For me, having a surgery date seemed to lift my spirit in ways I never imagined. It seemed to give me hope and I was able to endure the final days of the chemo better. Having a surgery date gave me a focus for healing. It represented the halfway mark in my illness. I saw the surgery as a midway point that would move me to the other side in my healing. Having a surgery date allowed me to give people a focus for their prayers. But most important, finally I could get rid of the cancer in my body.

Having a surgery date brings its own set of highs and lows. The high point of a surgery date is that you know that you are getting closer to getting rid of the cancer and being cancer-free. The low point of having a surgery date is that you begin to worry about the surgery in general. What if there are complications? What if they don't get all of the cancer? What if they find more cancer? There are tremendous mixed emotions once you get a surgery date. I had thought I would be happier than I was.

Generally by the time you get a surgery date, your body is so tired of the chemo treatment that you don't have a lot of time to focus on the negative aspects of the surgery. Receiving a surgery date will be anticlimactic and in many ways will raise even more questions. But like any journey, having a surgery date represents another step toward the final destination. In this journey called cancer, having a surgery date is another step toward recovery. It is a movement to the other side—the side of remission, the side toward a cancer-free life.

When Jesus invited his disciples to journey with him to the other side, it was an invitation to a time of rest from the toils of the journey. I received my surgery date as an invitation to go to the other side. I received an invitation to move to the other side of chemo. I received it as an invitation to move to the side of total healing. Finally, a surgery date! Finally, I can move forward toward total healing!

Dear Lord, thank you for bringing us thus far. Thank you for moving us toward the other side where total healing is possible. Thank you for your saving grace and your mercy that has sustained us. We receive this surgery date as a blessing and we ask that your perfect will be done. Amen.

God, I See You

GOD, I SEE YOU! During my illness, that became my mantra. I can truly say that each and every day God showed up in marvelous ways. I saw God in the big things like a day without much pain and an encouraging word from the doctor that my treatment was going as planned. I saw God in the strong prayers of my family and friends and the many acts of kindness from strangers. I saw God in the midst of worship and even as I preached the Word. But I expected to see God in those things. What amazed me was when I was made aware of the presence of God in the small things. I saw God when I woke up and realized that I had survived another day. I saw God on those days when I realized I had eaten something that I could taste. I saw God in my husband's smile and my daughter's hugs. I saw God everywhere. I became keenly aware of the quiet, awesome presence of God with me.

I have always been sensitive to the presence of the Eternal. I have always had a quiet way of communicating with God on a daily basis. I do not just pray but my life, every living moment, is a prayer. And this joy of living has often caused me to exclaim, *God, I see you! God, you're not hidden to me. God, I don't have to expect you to show up; you are ever-present.* My illness has made that come alive for me. I have learned to worship the God of the moment who comes and dwells in the midst of our pain and in the midst of every challenge. I don't want to ever stop being surprised by the awesome presence of God with me. I want to be able to say each and every day, *God, I see you!*

Dear Lord, thank you for your abiding presence. Lord, may you continue to show up in the everyday things of this life. We are encouraged to know that your promise to never leave us or forsake us is true. May we always be able to say, God, I see you! Amen.

I Can't Fix This

I'M A FIXER. I'm that kind of person who when confronted with a problem wants to fix it. I want to fix what's broken. I want to make it better. I'm the one who straightens the crooked picture or makes sure that the silver is lined up correctly on the table. I like things to be done right and all things to be in order. And I have also tended to deal with people in the same way. I don't like for people to be hurt; I don't like for people to be in need; I don't like for people to struggle. I want to make it better. Oh, of course, like most fixers, I have discovered that some things—most things—cannot be fixed by human hands; they require a miracle from God. But when trouble comes, the fixer in me is always the one jumping in there and trying to fix it. But with my cancer, I soon had to admit: *I can't fix this.*

My cancer made me feel helpless. And helpless is not a feeling I'm comfortable with. In fact, I hate feeling helpless. But cancer left me feeling helpless. I couldn't fix my cancer. I couldn't make it better. I couldn't reverse what was; I had to accept the fact that *I can't fix this.*

Women are natural fixers. It is for this exact reason that our family and friends rely so strongly on us. They know that when trouble comes, when things are not going well, we will do all we can to "fix it." But what happens when it's not about other people; what happens when it's about the "fixer"? What happens when the "fixer" can't "fix it"?

It's hard to admit that we can't "fix it." It's hard to admit that we don't have all the answers, that we don't have any answers. And cancer puts you in that hard place: *I can't fix this.* I had to deal with that. I had to accept the fact that some things are beyond my ability to fix. I had to learn to relinquish my place as fixer and allow God to do the fixing. It's hard to do that but it's critical to our complete healing.

Dear Lord, help us! No matter how hard we try, we can't fix what we're going through right now. Help us to turn this over completely to you. We need you to be our Divine Fixer in all things. We can't fix this, but we know you can. Amen.

Prayer Warriors

PRAYER WARRIORS ARE SPECIAL. They have a special call on their lives to intercede for others and to bring before the Lord the concerns and needs of others. They are consistent and vigilant in their work. There is no doubt in my mind that I am here because of the faithfulness of prayer warriors in my church family and throughout the country. They prayed for me and God heard their prayer. The prayers of the righteous do avail much!

I am blessed to belong to a church that has an active and committed Intercessory Prayer Ministry. They come to the sanctuary every day and pray for the concerns of the church and community. Once my illness was revealed, this became a major focus of the Intercessory Prayer Ministry. In addition, the church instituted a 24–7 prayer chain where members prayed for 15-minute intervals. So all day, every day, I was bathed in prayer. Just knowing that I was being prayed for in this way was extremely comforting.

Prayer warriors are warriors. I learned that firsthand. They pray as warriors who will not stop until they receive the victory. They prayed for healing. They prayed for every need, expecting to receive the victory. They prayed with a steadfastness and diligence that only God can give. On those occasions when I was privileged to hear the prayers of the prayer warriors, I was driven to tears and greatly humbled by their intense love and concern. The prayer warriors were awesome. It became commonplace to have persons call me and immediately go into a fervent prayer for my healing. It was not unusual to have people put me on an e-mail prayer list. I was listed on church prayer lists throughout the country. The prayer warriors rallied and kept my name before the Lord.

I thank God for the prayer warriors who do what they have been called to do so lovingly and so unassumingly on a daily basis. I have always appreciated the worth and power of prayer, but this season has opened my eyes to those with the gift of prayer—those who are used in a special way to bring healing and wholeness to others. Blessed are the prayer warriors; they are God's chosen vessels.

Dear Lord, thank you for the many persons who have prayed, and who continue to pray, for us. Thank you for the many prayer warriors who have kept us before you. As they have prayed for us, bless them and give them what they stand in need of. Lord, hear our prayers. Amen.

Cancer Doesn't Make It Better

LIFE IS STILL LIFE, WITH OR WITHOUT CANCER. Just because we have cancer doesn't mean that we don't get more trouble, more headaches, and more problems. For me, that was hard to take. I wanted to say, *I already have something to deal with; I have cancer. So life, you can't give me anything else!* But as we all know, life does not let up. Life does not slow down. Life does not always get better just because we have cancer. The car still needs to be fixed; we still need to complete the assignment we have been given; people still need answers from us; and there is still more than enough disappointment, frustration, and pain to deal with. Cancer doesn't make it better.

When I was first diagnosed, I had the luxury of ignoring life with all of its challenges. But as the illness progressed, life tapped me on the shoulder and reminded me that it would not be ignored. And to insure that it would not be ignored, things started to happen. People died; things broke down; things didn't fall into place; people were annoying; you name it, it happened. Life began to go on and it was still life as it had been before cancer. Cancer didn't make it better.

For some reason, I thought that life would sympathize with me, just as everyone else was doing. But life was not impressed with me and my concerns. I was not some special person who needed to be handled with kid gloves. Life was often cruel, unrelenting, and uninterested. Cancer did not make life more pleasant, kinder, or gentler. Cancer did not make it better. So I did with life what I had always done with life: I took away life's power and put life under the control of my God who, in spite of how life treated me, has always been loving, gracious, caring, compassionate, and kind.

Dear Lord, thank you for your loving kindness in spite of the challenges of this life. Help us to deal with all of those things we must endure as a part of this life. Without you, we don't know what we would do. Thank you for bringing us over and through. Amen.

The Dishes Still Have to Be Washed

THE DISHES STILL HAVE TO BE DONE. I'm tired; I've been at work all day; I have cancer; but the dishes still need to be done. I remember that day when I came home after finally being able to resume most of my previous schedule to be confronted by a sink full of dishes. My daughter was at basketball practice, my husband was on an appointment, and there was a sink full of dishes. *When did this happen? When did we return to life as usual? Did they forget to send me the memo?* I remember thinking all of that as I changed my clothes and returned to the kitchen to wash the dishes. Whether I'm ready or not, the dishes have to be done. Things can no longer be ignored or passed on to others. We have to live and do what has to be done and what we can do while we can do it.

Dishes—a common reminder that I am a part of a family where I have assumed some responsibilities. I am a part of a team and together we do what needs to be done that we all might be comfortable. For months, my family had done double duty. They had taken on all of my pieces without complaint or displaying any sense of burden. But the dishes needed to be washed. I knew that if I left them, someone would come home and wash them. I also knew that someone, like me, would be adding to an already full day. But the dishes needed to be washed now. In spite of cancer, the dishes still have to be washed.

During times of illness, the household is disrupted. It is during those times that we realize how the household runs. We appreciate what each person does and how what they do is for the good of all. I'm sure that my daughter and husband realized my valuable role during my illness. Yes, they did all of the things that needed to be done. They washed the dishes—maybe not the way I would have or even to my satisfaction. But nevertheless, the dishes got washed.

It was interesting how on that day a sink full of dirty dishes called me back to the routine things of life. As I stared down at the dishes, God spoke, *Pat, the dishes still have to washed.* So I smiled and washed the dishes, grateful that God spared me to wash them one more time.

Dear Lord, bless those of us with cancer as we return to our daily duties. Bless us as we clean, wash, and fulfill other household responsibilities. Continue to give us strength. Help us to see you in all that we are called to do, no matter how mundane it may seem. Amen.

Me Time

WHEN I WAS FIRST DIAGNOSED, I GREATLY APPRECIATED AND YEARNED FOR THE PRESENCE OF OTHERS. It was so comforting to have people around me to pray with me, to listen to me share about my progress, to reassure me that God would be faithful and would eventually heal me. God was faithful to send an abundance of people. At home, at church, wherever I went there were people, people, and more people! I needed some "me time." I needed some time to be alone with me and to do what I wanted to do without anyone being concerned about me or talking to me or asking me anything. And it was hard to claim this "me time" because I did not want to offend all of the kind people who had put their life on hold to care for me and to be there for me.

I decided to develop my own plan for "me time." It started with my decision to go to my radiation treatments alone. Although my husband was faithful to go to every doctor's appointment, every chemo session with me, and the first radiation session with me, I decided that I would attend the rest of the sessions alone. It was draining. It was hard, but it gave me a moment to be alone with myself and to deal with myself about what was happening to my body. I just needed to be alone; I needed to be left alone for some hours during the day.

Once I got everyone to allow me to go for treatments alone, I ventured further. I started driving again. Ah, sweet freedom! Now I could go places after my treatment. So some days I drove to the park and sat on the bench and read. Some days I just drove down lonely country roads and allowed my mind to be at peace. Once I was even able to sneak into a matinee movie without being recognized. I'm sure my family and friends would have been horrified to know what I was doing. So it became my little secret. I just needed some "me time."

God always knows what we need and desire. So God used the women in my church to present me with a supply of gift certificates for massages and spa days. And I discovered a masseuse who specialized in massage therapy for cancer patients. So faithfully, once a week, I would allow the gentle massage to pamper me and soothe me and allow me to be refreshed and revived.

"Me time" is crucial for those of us with cancer. We need time to relax on our own terms. We need time to be stress-free and time to pamper ourselves. We need time when we can put our illness aside and laugh and do absolutely nothing. We deserve some "me time" and we have to claim it for ourselves.

Dear Lord, thank you for the quiet moments and the time when we can be alone to gather our thoughts. Bless all of those who need space to think things through. Provide "me time" to those in need and give them the courage to claim it for themselves. Amen.

Ain't I a Woman?

I REMEMBER WHEN THE DOCTOR TOLD ME I WOULD HAVE TO HAVE A MASTECTOMY. They would have to remove my right breast because the size of the tumor was too large to do a lumpectomy. The mastectomy would save my life and give me a better chance of the cancer not returning. Given my choices, I had no problems with undergoing a mastectomy. But now the surgery is over and I have to live with the decision that has been made. Now I lay in a hospital bed heavily bandaged on my right side, knowing that I am minus a right breast.

There is something about losing a body part. This was my breast and now I no longer have it. Already my body feels differently. How will my body look when the bandage is taken off? While in the hospital, my family and friends came and we laughed and shared together and everyone was very careful not to get caught looking at the side where my breast had been.

I have never been overly possessed about my body. Growing up, I was skinny and never had big legs or breasts. I never defined myself by the size of my body parts. I never saw my body parts as the sum total of who I am. I always had a healthy, positive outlook about myself as a woman. I was never jealous about other women's body parts and I was very comfortable in my own skin. I had not thought about my breasts since I was in junior high when I did the tissue in my bra thing because my breasts were so slow in developing. But I'm a grown woman now who has lost a right breast. And surprisingly, that thought began to play with my mind. *Ain't I a woman?*

I remember the day when I could finally take the bandage off. I kept it on as long as I could, but finally I knew I had to take it off and look at my body without a right breast. I had been adamant about not wanting breast reconstruction, but now I wondered if I had made the right decision. How would I feel about a body that may look deformed and disfigured?

I remember going into my dressing room outside of the shower in our bathroom and sitting on the vanity stool as I slowly unwrapped the dressing. I remember looking at the line across my chest where my breast had been. It looked so strange but certainly not horrible, not repulsive. I really can't describe how I felt. As the tears began to flow, I felt a little sad, but not devastated. I didn't feel less than a woman but I felt different as a woman. It's hard to explain. I remember rubbing the spot, comparing it to the other side where my left breast was. For a fleeting moment I wondered how my husband would feel about this body without a right breast. *Ain't I a woman?*

While I was thinking all of these thoughts at the same time, sitting naked before a full-length mirror in my dressing room, God spoke. It was a gentle reassuring Spirit that rose up on the inside of me that day and reassured me that I am still the woman God created. I am more than my body parts. I am completely whole by the grace of Almighty God. *Ain't I a woman? Yes, I am!*

Dear Lord, bless all of the women who have undergone a mastectomy. Be with them in the choices of reconstruction or not. Lord, help us as women to know that we have been created in your wonderful image and we are much more than our body parts. Make us whole by your grace. Amen.

Chemotherapy

I ENDURED EIGHT ROUNDS OF CHEMOTHERAPY. There are no kind words for chemotherapy—it is something that has to be endured. It takes all of your strength and takes your body through changes you never imagined. I had asked those who had gone through chemotherapy about it. No one had anything good to say about it except that it was something to be endured. So I began my four-month ordeal with chemotherapy expecting the worst.

For me chemotherapy was not half as bad as everyone said it would be. It was certainly not a piece of cake, but it was tolerable. At my first visit, I was extremely anxious, but the doctor and nurses patiently walked me through the procedure. I was amazed that I felt fine afterward and didn't experience any terrible pain or fatigue. The first four rounds of chemo involved a drug which made me lose my hair and made me a little nauseous. But the medication eased it and generally by day two I was fine. The most difficult thing was losing my ability to taste. I had a hard time finding something that I could taste. The minute I'd find something, I would soon discover that I could not taste it either. Going out to eat with my family was nearly impossible. I could not be in the kitchen because the smells would upset my stomach or cause me to lose my appetite. It was difficult but surprisingly tolerable. Before I knew it, I had reached my fourth and what I thought would be my final dose of chemo.

When I was told that I would have to take four more rounds of chemo using a different drug, I was devastated. While the chemo has been tolerable, I wanted to be done with it. I was depressed for two days. But I was determined to endure the last four rounds as well as I had the first four rounds. For whatever reason, the second level of chemo affected me severely. It agitated my arthritis and made sleeping at night almost impossible. I had to take pain pills at night to help me sleep and after each chemo round, by day three I was unable to get out of bed. I was literally out of it for about seven days and would begin to feel better about a week prior to the next treatment. I began to walk with a cane because my balance was so affected. It was horrible. All of the horror stories became true for me. I lost 20 pounds because I could not eat during this period. My nails turned black and I lost feeling in the tips of my fingers and toes.

The day I finished chemo was a blessed day. There were times that I felt if the cancer didn't kill me, surely the chemo would.

Chemo teaches you to walk by faith and not by sight because if you rely on how you feel, you will lose all hope. There were days during my last rounds of chemo treatment that I felt that I would not make it. But God was at work in the chemo to destroy cancer cells in my body. I thank God for bringing me through. I thank God for the prayers of the faithful. I thank God that what I see in my body as a result of the chemo is only temporary. My nails and hair and strength will return. Restoration will take place because the God whom we serve promises to restore what has been torn down and to renew what has been destroyed. My body belongs to God and he will restore it in due time.

Dear Lord, thank you for giving us the strength to endure chemo. Renew our bodies and make us whole again. We trust you and thank you that the chemo is not destroying us but is killing the cancer. Lord, keep us in your care and may your perfect will be done. Amen.

Thank God for Family

WE OFTEN TAKE FAMILY FOR GRANTED. But during times of sickness and death, we can always count on family. My family was awesome during my illness. Once they got over the initial shock and devastation, they rallied around me in marvelous ways. All of the fractions came together with one purpose: *We have to take care of Ann* (Ann is what my family calls me). I was not surprised; yet I was very surprised at the same time. Our family is small and very busy and spread out throughout the country. So to see them as this "ministering team" was simply amazing.

My husband was truly the "general." He controlled everything and, when necessary, kept everyone at bay. He kept me in bed, took me to appointments, fussed with care providers, did the household chores, rubbed my aching body, listened to my cries, and was my advocate in all things. Once my daughter was told, she stayed close, was generous with the hugs, and always inquired about my needs. My little brother became the "big brother" with his gentle concern, forever urging me to take care of myself. He quietly took over in the total care of our mother, assuring me that he would take care of her so that I could concentrate on getting well.

My aunt and her daughter were like sisters to me, always doing the little things that others tended to forget were needed. They brought food and sat for hours on end at the hospital and at the house. Cousins came, called, did what they could, and sent their love. My family was awesome. The miles meant nothing. My nephew traveled from Fredericksburg, bringing me meditation books and healing scriptures to read. My family from Philadelphia came for weekends and called daily. They came in carloads—cousins and aunts and their children. Everywhere there was family. All they needed to know was that I was sick. While I was in the hospital, my hospital suite was always filled with family and friends.

My mother-in-law is a twenty-year cancer survivor. Her friendship and testimony was a tremendous blessing. She shared all of her pamphlets from her journey. Although she's sick and undergoing dialysis, she never fails to call and encourage me. My sisters-in law were gracious and kind, never forgetting to keep me lifted up in prayer. I thank God for family. Without the love and care of family, this journey would be impossible. Whenever I feel like giving up, I think of the fact that my family loves me and they have invested in my healing in many marvelous ways. The love of family is priceless!

Dear Lord, bless the families of those with cancer. Thank you for the love and care that these families provide. Thank you for their great sacrifice during this journey. Lord, we pray for our families today. Bless them and give then all that they stand in need of as they care for us. Amen.

Try This . . .

TRY THIS . . . THAT'S HOW MANY OF THE CONVERSATIONS BEGIN WHEN PEOPLE HEAR THAT YOU'RE SICK. Everyone has a cure; everyone knows what will make you feel better; everyone feels comfortable offering a plan of action for your healing. I can't begin to tell you about all the remedies that have been offered to me, all by well-meaning people. I can't tell you how many times I have found myself in a corner while someone told me exactly what would cure me instantly. I've been given pills, all kinds of juices, mysterious mixtures that came from "grandma's recipe," and some potions that bordered on the illegal. Sickness in the African American community inspires creativity and connects us to our heritage in Africa like nothing else can do. I thank God for everyone who cared enough about me to send, write down, or give me their healing remedy.

One of my friends died of cancer in 1992. I remember talking with her one day and she disclosed that she was trying some Eastern treatments that had not been approved here in the United States. She was going to a doctor who was doing special cleansings coupled with acupuncture and administering Eastern medicine. Her family was furious and had cautioned her against continuing to see him. She asked me about it. Not knowing that I would find myself in the same position, I encouraged her to listen to God for herself and to remember that in the final analysis, it was her body and she was free to make the decisions that pleased her. Now that I'm faced with the same decisions, I must admit that the advice we give to others is not always the advice we take ourselves. But I found that I still believe that we have to hear God for ourselves when it comes to the cures we entertain. Every remedy is not for us, even if it did heal someone else.

One of things I came to know from talking to my mother-in-law who was a twenty-year cancer survivor is that cancer is a very personal disease. There are some common aspects for all persons who have breast cancer, but it's different for each person. How we react to chemo is different, even when the same drug is used. How radiation affects our bodies is different. Every remedy is different for different people. It's hard to determine what will work across-the-board. So I had to pray hard and rely on God to lead me. I decided to rely on what my doctors recommended and to trust God to do the rest.

So I would accept every remedy with a smile and thank the person for caring enough about me to offer it. I never promised that I would take it, but I promised I would consult God and my doctor and follow their advice for me. They were always pleased that I would consider it. This allowed people to bless me without my offending their efforts. But it also freed me from feeling the need to try everything that was presented to me and running the risk of hindering my progress. *Try this . . .* Maybe, maybe not.

Dear Lord, thank you for the gift of medicine and procedures to heal your people. As you cure us of our diseases, give us the courage to trust the doctors and care providers you have called to work on your behalf. Continue to bring forth new and innovative medicines and give more options for healing. Lord, we thank you for every remedy that has been offered in love. Amen.

My Testimony

I AM BLESSED TO BE A PART OF A CHURCH WHERE TESTIMONIES ARE NOT ONLY A PART OF THE SUNDAY MORNING WORSHIP EXPERIENCE, THEY ARE ESSENTIAL TO IT. We believe that it is by the testimonies of the saints that the body is strengthened. We have been blessed to hear people give their testimony of being delivered from drugs and alcohol, having God put their marriages back together, being healed of diseases, and having God restore joy and renew a sense of excitement for life. These testimonies have thrilled me, driven me to tears, and sent me shouting across the pulpit. As I have taught the congregation, I firmly believe that you can't have a testimony without going through the test. But I also know that a testimony should leave the congregation excited about God and hopeful that what God has done for you, God will do for them.

It took me a while to finally give my testimony with regard to the cancer. The congregation had heard so many of my testimonies: how God saved me, how God brought me back to the church, how God allowed be to leave my government job for full-time ministry. But they had not heard my testimony about cancer. For many my presence was the testimony. It was truly amazing to have missed only one Sunday from the pulpit. Many of the deacons and those close to me had heard me regurgitating in my bathroom prior to service. Many had seen me bent over and exhausted after service. But they still had not heard my testimony.

A testimony is personal and freeing. Our testimony strips us of all pretense and moves people to see God. Our testimony is really our greatest and most lasting gift to the body of believers. And as a pastor I knew that the people wanted to hear their pastor's testimony. They wanted to know what God was doing and what promises God had made to me. But although I knew that, I could not give my testimony until it was released in me to give it to them.

I gave my testimony during the *worship and praise* portion of the service on a 1st Sunday, the Sunday when our congregation has communion and the day that we call "homecoming." This is the Sunday when all the saints try to be present in worship and, therefore, worship on the 1st Sunday tends to be filled to capacity. This 1st Sunday was no different. The congregation was excited about worship and expecting to be blessed mightily by the presence of the Lord.

My testimony was simple and direct: *I have been abundantly blessed by the Lord. Although I have just started this journey to total healing, I am healed by the power of Almighty God. Today I stand before you as a miracle—as an example of what God can do in spite of the odds. My soul rejoices in God because if it had not been for the Lord on my side, I don't know where I would be . . .* I can't remember all of what I said. All I know is that people heard that God is a healer. They heard that sickness is the common denominator for us all; it is no respecter of persons. They heard that God loves us all and this God deserves our total praise!

Dear Lord, we could do without the test, but we thank you for the testimony. We see your divine hand in our healing and deliverance. May our testimony inspire others to trust you and serve you. May our very lives be a testimony of your grace and mercy shown toward us. Amen.

The Prayers of the Saints

PRAYER IS POWERFUL! One of the things that has sustained me during this illness has been the prayers of the saints. People throughout the city and the country have been praying for me. There are special prayer chains that have been set up and my church is praying daily. These prayers have been a source of comfort in ways that I cannot fully comprehend. Just to know that people are praying for you does wonders for your healing. When I first became ill, I was reluctant to tell others or to solicit their prayers. But once that yoke was broken and people were freed to pray for me, it released a special kind of energy that is hard to explain. It brought to me a new kind of hope and it inspired my own personal prayer life.

The prayers of the saints have been special to me. I've had people come to church for the express reason to pray for me. One Sunday after church, two prayer warriors from our city made their way across town to pray the prayer of healing for me. It was a timely and needed visit because this was a Sunday that had been particularly difficult for me. While I had been able to preach that Sunday, I was in extreme pain and walking with the aid of a cane. I was drained by the conclusion of the service and resting in my office preparing to go home. When one of the greeters told me that there were two women who were waiting patiently outside, desiring to see me, I knew who they were and asked that they come back to see me. They came with a mission in mind—to pray the prayer of healing over me. As they began to bask me with love and prayer, I could feel the return of strength and energy. I am eternally grateful to God for his ambassadors whom he continues to send to encourage and to pray for my healing.

In another instance, I went to minister at a church for the pastor's anniversary. After I had ministered to the congregation, the pastor asked that I would come forward for the church to pray for me. As I sat and people surrounded me, the church prayed for my healing. Once again, the ministry of prayer was a blessing that energized and healed me at a particular point of need.

Prayer has been my mainstay during this journey. The prayers of my church family have been a constant. The children of the church have prayed for me. And there is nothing like the prayers of children. In their innocence, in their loving touches as they rallied around me, there was an amazing feeling of the presence of God. I felt the divine touch of God through the children in a powerful way. Prayer is indeed powerful.

During this time, I have learned to allow prayer to carry me. I thank God for the prayers of the saints. I thank God for the gift of prayer that others have so freely offered to me. I thank God for the prayers of those who don't even know me but are lifting me up on the wings of prayer. Their prayers are keeping my mind and my heart, and their prayers are healing my body. I wake up every morning encouraged and blessed because I know that someone is praying for me.

Dear Lord, thank you for the prayers of the saints. We are so grateful for those you have been inspired to pray for us. Thank you for hearing their prayers even when we cannot pray for ourselves. Lord, we are blessed by the healing power of prayer. Thank you for hearing our prayers and continuing to answer day by day. Amen.

The Class Reunion

I GRADUATED FROM ARMSTRONG HIGH SCHOOL IN RICHMOND, VIRGINIA, IN 1965. We are about to celebrate our 40th class reunion. When I first received the notice of the events, I had not been diagnosed with cancer and I was looking forward to attending and seeing all of my old classmates. But once the diagnosis came, I was reluctant to respond indicating that I would attend. I waited until the last possible minute to indicate that I would be attending. In fact, it was only after they placed me on the program that I decided that I would attend.

Class reunions bring with them their own set of questions: What will I wear? How will I look compared to my fellow classmates? Have I gained too much weight? Because most of my graduating class has stayed close, those questions never seemed important for me as I prepared for all of the prior reunions. But as I prepared for this reunion, the questions became real and I wrestled with them. I didn't want to be the center of attention and have my friends and classmates pity me and focus on my illness.

I decided to wear a hat to the dinner although I had chosen to wear a bald head during my illness. I felt this would allow me to blend in better and allow the conversation to be about other things besides my illness. I had a wonderful time. The night was positive and upbeat. I got to reminisce and laugh about old times with friends whom I had not seen for years. There were some moments when I felt a little awkward. I was a little anxious when

I first entered the room, walking with a cane. But as I began to greet people and hug people and talk to people, I felt at home. As I looked around the room, I thanked God for all of us making it to see our 40th class reunion. I rejoiced to see couples who were still together and to see classmates who had not changed over all of the years. It was good to remember that although we had all gone through a lot over the years, we were all a testimony to the goodness of the Lord.

I was so glad that I went to my 40th class reunion. I was able to see the power of God in a marvelous way. As we shared in the Armstrong Trivia Game, we could laugh about the good times we shared so long ago. As we looked at pictures of ourselves from 1965, we could be thankful for who we are today. As we remembered those who have gone on, we could be grateful for a new opportunity to live. I am so glad that I went. I'm glad that I did not allow cancer to stop me from the joy of being with friends. I'm grateful to God for allowing me to see those who, like myself, have endured life's unexpected circumstances and who have survived.

The class reunion was a great blessing. It renewed my hope and strength. I felt beautiful and I felt loved. It was a safe place for me. I was blessed to see walking miracles. I was blessed to hear about how God has blessed over the years. I was blessed to know that friendships do last. I left feeling good about who God has allowed each of us to become by God's power and grace. I left looking forward to the 50th class reunion. I certainly intend to strive to be present for it.

Dear Lord, thank you for allowing me to see my 40th class reunion. Thank you for how you have blessed my classmates and my friends. Lord, help us to celebrate every reunion as a gift from you. Help us to know that you hold the key to the future. Keep us in your care and help us to enjoy the blessing of fellowship with one another. Amen.

I Don't See Death When I Look at You

FRIENDS CAN BE SO CANDID. Friends don't hold back anything; they tell it like it is. And one of my friends said to me with a great deal of sincerity: *I don't see death when I look at you.* One of my friends had heard about my illness. He had called offering prayer, but he had not seen me. So on his way home from the Hampton Ministers' Conference, he decided to come through Richmond and take me to lunch. It was good to see him and we enjoyed the time together catching one another up with regard to spouses and children. We talked about our ministries and what God was leading us to do next. But throughout the lunch, I didn't miss the glances at me as if looking for some kind of sign of imminent death.

There is only so much idle chit-chat and we both knew it, so finally my friend Thomas looked at me directly and said, *I don't see death when I look at you.* The comment floored me. I didn't really know how to feel about what he said. *Am I supposed to say thank you? Am I supposed to feel flattered? Who said I looked like death?* While all of those questions were swirling in my head, my friend rushed to explain. He had been led to believe I was indeed dying. The rumor mill had me on my deathbed. He was pleasantly surprised when he talked to me on the phone and was even more encouraged when I was able to meet him for lunch. But he said he still didn't know what to expect when he saw me. And when he saw me, the only way he knew to describe it was to say, *I don't see death when I look at you.*

I had to deal with that statement. Every cancer patient does. How do we look to others? What do they see on us? Do they see death or do they see life? I was grateful that my friend was candid enough to speak it out of his mouth. And I was grateful that he *didn't* see death when he looked at me. But I could not help wonder, what if he *had* seen death when he looked at me? Would he have told me? Is that what people are doing when we catch them staring at us? Are they trying to determine if we're dying? I don't know. I have to not rush to misunderstanding every look and comment.

On that day, I was blessed to know that I looked normal, not like one who was dying. I don't know what death looks like. I don't know what death feels like. What I do know is that regardless of how we look, God is still a healer. And God's divine healing looks and feels wonderful!

Dear Lord, thank you for every day of life. Thank you for restoring us day by day. Thank you for giving us the strength to live and not die in spite of the odds we have been given. Thank you for every encouraging word given by friends. We receive it as coming from you. Amen.

The Comfort of Friends

WHEN YOU'RE SICK, YOU SOMETIMES FORGET HOW COMFORTING THE COMPANY OF FRIENDS CAN BE. Just being around good friends with no agendas, no questions, but just a lot of laughter and foolishness can bring healing to your soul. I was blessed to have many comforting girlfriends whose sole purpose was to spend quality time with me on a consistent basis during this journey.

I have many wonderful girlfriends who in spite of their academic credentials don't mind acting silly and enjoying a good laugh together. During my sickness, it was wonderful to be "kidnapped" by these friends from time to time. They would come and take me out for long lunches filled with giggles and craziness. Those times allowed us to leave behind the high expectations of our students and colleagues. We were free to be ourselves in ways that were impossible in our career setting. For a few minutes we could be free to just be "girlfriends."

I don't remember exactly when Alison, Katie, and I became friends. I so admired their academic prowess as womanist theologians. They were my s/heroes. But I found that in spite of who they were academically, they were wonderful *sista girlfriends*, especially during this season in my life. Each of them had an easy smile, a quick wit, and a compassionate spirit. I felt comfortable around them and felt as if I had known them for years. There was no pretense, just the comforting presence of good friends. I cherished those days of fun with friends. It allowed me to appreciate the blessing that comes through those whom God has placed in our lives as dear friends.

I was blessed to have many friends, old and new. Like the Girl Scouts song says: *Make new friends but keep the old; one is silver and the other is gold.* So like my newfound friends, I found comfort in those friends who had been with me through the years. Once I was able to get out, I began to go out to dinner with four of my elementary school girlfriends every second Wednesday of the month. The hours of reminiscing was comforting and lifted my spirits immensely. They created a bond to see me through the hard times of my illness.

The friends who brought me comfort are too numerous to name individually, but each one was my personal angel. They prayed, sent cards, sent funny gifts, came by, called, wrote letters, and sent me messages through e-mail and Facebook. I was greatly comforted by all this "to do" about me. I so appreciate that it was all done with the ease that only friends can possess. I discovered that for my friends, loving and caring for me was comfortable and natural for them. And this fact alone was very comforting to me.

Dear Lord, thank you for the many friends you have placed in our lives. They have been a great source of comfort to us and we appreciate all that they do. We know this is your doing. When we think of friends, we realize that there is no friend like you. Thank you, Lord Jesus, for being our friend. Amen.

When Everyone Else Sleeps

EVERY CANCER PATIENT KNOWS ABOUT THOSE MIDNIGHT HOURS WHEN EVERYONE ELSE HAS GONE TO SLEEP. The days are filled with appointments, routine activities, and doctors' visits, and there are people all around you. The days are packed and the pace is such that you just get carried along by the natural order of things. There's not a lot of time to ponder, to stop, to question, or to feel sorry for yourself. During the day, living through the day is your sole purpose. But once night falls, and you find yourself approaching the end of the day, your mood changes. For me, night signaled that soon everyone else would be asleep and I would be alone to deal with my own feelings. I found that to be frightening.

My husband is a heavy sleeper, and probably more so given all that he was doing to keep things going. It became my routine to allow him to fall asleep and try for about an hour to be lulled into sleep by his snoring. But every night I found that no matter how I tried to go to sleep, sleep eluded me. So I would slip silently out of bed and go into my study and sit for hours with the lights out and think about where I was and what I felt God was doing with me. There was no crying and no praying. This was a season of quietly being alone with myself and being alone with God without talking to God. This became my ritual—silence, aloneness, darkness, and stillness.

There is something sacred about the stillness of a house late at night. In the past, God had used this time to speak to me and to give direction about my ministry and to lead me to pray for others. But now this sacred stillness has taken on new meaning and purpose for me. And I have to work through it. It's frightening to not pray. It's frightening to have no real thoughts that matter. It's hard to just sit and wait and then get up and go back to bed. But this is where God has me and even though we're not speaking, I know God is there with me.

This cancer journey is not under our control. Nothing is like it was before. Those things that we found comforting before may be disturbingly different now. When everyone else sleeps, we get a chance to sit with those differences. But even those differences are not devoid of the blessings of God.

Dear Lord, thank you for being with us when everyone else sleeps. As we struggle to understand what is happening to our bodies and even to us, we ask for your reassurance. Bless us in the quiet, in the stillness of the night. Amen.

The Pastor's Call

EVERY PASTOR NEEDS A PASTOR. How many times had I been told that in seminary and by older seasoned pastors? But my pastor has yet to call me. I had been told that my name was on the prayer list at my former church where I served before planting my present church. Many members had called, but the pastor has not called. I knew that the pastor was busy and had only a year earlier returned to the pulpit himself after a kidney transplant. But he has not called.

My illness helped me to appreciate what the comfort of the pastor does for those who are sick within the body. As a pastor, it helped me to not underestimate the power of the pastor's call and the pastor's prayer. Even for those like myself who are able to pray for themselves and who have many people praying for them; there is nothing like the ministry of the pastor. I need the pastor to call me—not the deacons, not the missionaries, but the pastor.

The call came when I was least expecting it. In fact, I had concluded that the pastor would not call because of his schedule and the things he might be going through physically. But one day as I sat in the recliner watching TV or allowing TV to watch me, the phone rang: *Hi, Pat. How are you doing?* . . . I was reduced to tears and immediately I began to share everything that I had been holding in, things that you can only tell your pastor. The conversation was so compassionate and kind. I hung up grateful for the call and thankful that I had such a pastor.

That moment shaped my ministry. It confirmed the reason why pastoral visitation and care is critical to the life of the church. There are some things that only the pastor can do. While everyone else's prayers and ministry are appreciated, there is indeed something special about the pastor's care. I promised to never forget that fact in my own ministry.

For all of those who are sick, let us always inform our pastor concerning what we need and desire from them. Realizing that pastors are human, let us remember to never assume that the pastor's absence indicates a lack of love and compassion. Let us pray for our pastor as they pray for and minister to our needs.

Dear Lord, bless our pastors as they comfort us. Give them the strength to care for those who are sick and in need of care. Send others to help them in this compassionate work. As they call, visit, and pray for us, may we also pray for them as well. Continue to use them in a mighty way. Amen.

Radiation

WELL, THE CHEMOTHERAPY IS OVER AND THE SURGERY IS OVER. Now it's time for radiation. I was already physically exhausted, and I was not looking forward to beginning another round of grueling, draining procedures. By the time my husband and I got to the appointment, I was not in a good place. After the tour, the nurse sat with us to determine the days and time for my radiation sessions. As she was talking, I experienced the greatest level of sadness I had felt since my treatment began. It was as if every doubt and every fear converged at once and settled in my spirit.

My husband and I rode home in complete silence. I knew my husband could feel my sadness, but he allowed me the space to deal with it in silence. Once I got home, the faucet was turned on and the tears began to flow, non-stop. My husband tried to console me as best he could, but at that point in time, I was inconsolable. But as always, God gave me the strength to move beyond that moment of despair. So on the next Monday, I went to my first radiation session—alone. I was driving now and feeling reasonably well, so I told my husband that I didn't want him or anyone else to go with me to radiation. Reluctantly, he complied.

One of the first things I discovered about radiation is that while it appears to be a simple, short process (no more than 20 minutes), it is quite draining physically and emotionally. It was challenging to lift and keep my arms over my head, to tilt my body in the exact position they desired and not move, to tolerate the little color-marking tattoos on my body. My skin turned black and the burn marks never fully faded away.

Radiation had its own challenges, but I quickly got used to the process. There was a radiation team that served a small group of diverse patients who were drawn into a common community based on their receiving radiation at the same time every week. We came to know each other by face; there was really no time for chatting. You came in, got checked in, immediately went to the locker room, changed your clothes, and came to the end of the hall and waited for the person in front of you to leave the radiation room so you could enter. You saw the person in front of you, and after your session you saw the person behind you. These two people became your anchor people. The person in front of me always had an encouraging word as we passed in the hall. The man behind me was always leaning against the wall as I exited the radiation room. He never spoke but would always give me a very small nod. Eventually the nod became a small smile and a soft hello. I found myself cheering them on. I was frantic if I didn't see one of them for a few days. They became my sense of reality. If they were still there, all was well.

When my time was up, I concluded radiation with a genuine sense of great relief. I felt wonderful to have come to this end of the road. I left wondering how my fellow survivors were doing. I continue to pray for them, that they too are being healed.

Dear Lord, thank you for getting us through radiation. Thank you for all of the technicians and those who lovingly guided us through it. Bless those who are on the journey with me, in different stages of their own illnesses. Keep us all in your perfect care. Amen.

Trading Places

MY MOTHER IS EIGHTY YEARS OLD WITH THE ONSET OF DEMENTIA. My father died two years ago and since his death, my mother's dementia has progressed. My brother and I have committed ourselves to caring for our mother and keeping her in the home that she and my father shared for the last 30 years. This journey with my mother had been interesting, to say the least. It's been like trading places. My mother, who always took care of me, is now dependent upon my brother and me to take care of her. We have traded places.

Trading places with my mother has not been easy for me. To see the strong woman, who alongside my father was the backbone of our family, being cared for like a baby is heartbreaking. To see her lose her ability to walk and to speak in complete sentences and to know those of us who are her closest loved ones is devastating. She now calls me "Mama." She depends on me to feed her and to clothe her and to speak up for her. I now have to do what she did for me and my brother—I have to be "Mommy."

Trading places is hard because it denotes a restructure of the family. The people we expect to be in certain places shift and are no longer where we have come to expect them to be. Over time there is a lot of trading places that can take place within our families. With my illness, I feel that I'm trading places again. My mother, even in her present state of dementia, knows that I'm sick. She reaches out to hug me, she babbles, trying to talk to me, perhaps to tell me that everything will be alright. During my illness, my brother says my mother is getting stronger and she even calls my name. Perhaps, somewhere in the recesses of her mind, she's trying to take back her role as mother and take care of me.

There's been some trading of places with regard to my daughter. She's no longer so clingy and dependent on "Mommy." She's coming into her own and on occasion is my "Mommy" as she takes care of me. At first, like my mother, I resisted this shift in the order of things; I resisted this trading of places that subtly occurred without my permission. But all of these things are of God. God calls us to step in when and where we are needed. God knows our future and God calls us to be prepared to do what we have seen done by those who went before us.

I thank God for the opportunity and the ability to trade places with my mother. I count it a privilege to care for my mother in her time of need. In doing so, I have been enormously blessed and in the process have been reassured that God will have someone trade places with me when needed.

Dear Lord, bless all of us who are caregivers for others. During those times when we have to take on the role that others have played in our lives, give us the strength to follow their lead and to be for them what they have been for us. Help us and give us the strength to care for others as others are caring for us. Amen.

Against All Odds...
I WILL NOT DIE BUT LIVE

*I will not die but live, and will proclaim
what the L*ORD *has done.*
PSALM 118:17, NIV

Have you ever had all the odds stacked against you? Have you ever been at the point where you didn't just *think* you weren't going to make it but you *knew* you weren't going to make it? Have you ever had somebody give up on you? Have you been at that point where you were so low that you thought you would surely die? If you answered yes to any of these questions then I just want to say to you this morning, Welcome to the club, because all of us have been there. All of us have been there in one form or another. All of us have been there to one degree or another. All of us have had all the odds stacked against us at one time or another. But I've come with some good news today. To those who have had the odds against you and those who have the odds against you right now, I want to say that you can make it against all odds. That's what this text is all about.

When I read this text it just leaped up in my spirit because I meet so many people day after day whose spirits have been broken because they're working against the odds. Their spirits are just broken and they are convinced that they cannot make it. There are people who are doing battle with all kinds of problems, all kind of trials, and all kind of tribulations. But in spite of that God wants us to know you can make it against all odds. Just turn to somebody and say, "You can make it against all odds."

When we approach this text we find that here are some Jews and they are singing a song of deliverance because in spite of the odds, they have come through victoriously. In spite of the odds that they would never see their homeland again they have been returned to their homeland and things have come back together again. These are Jews who have been to the bottom; they had been in captivity in Babylon where they were forced to give up everything they knew, everything that was comfortable for them. They have had their spirits broken to the point that they couldn't even sing the songs of Zion anymore. But in spite of all of that, in spite of all the odds that were against them, they had been restored to their lands, returned to their homes, and now they are at the point of building the new temple. They made it against all odds.

This is a psalm of thanksgiving. Psalm 118 is a song of victory, a psalm of triumph, a psalm of hope, and it is also a psalm of confidence. It is a psalm of confidence because the psalmist says, *"I shall not die, but live, And declare the works of the LORD."* In other words, I can make it and I'm gonna make it against all odds.

Many of us have come today against all odds. Some of us have come today right in the middle of the eye of the storm. Some of us have come wrestling, wondering if it's ever going to get any better. And if you haven't come in this condition you've come knowing somebody in this condition, because all of us know somebody who's going through something right now.

Many of us as African Americans are going through something right now and it appears that the odds are against us. Many of our families are going through something right now and it appears that the odds are against us. Many of our children are going through something right now and it appears that the odds are against them. Many of us are just going through and through and through and it appears that the odds keep stacking up against us. But this text serves to remind us that it is possible to make it against all odds. It's possible to survive against all odds. It's possible to live life victoriously against all odds. This text serves to remind us that it's a matter of not only of our head (you know we often say, "You know you got to get your head right—it's all in your thinking"), but it's also a matter of our heart; we have to get our hearts right too. If we're going to survive we have to play a part in our own survival, and I don't know about you, but many of us are defeated because we have given up in our spirit. We have just given over our willpower and we don't think we can make it anymore, but we've got to get it in our head and in our heart that victory is possible. The psalm writer reminds us that we have to take personal responsibility for our victory; we have to take personal responsibility that we are going to survive; we have to say deep down in our soul, *I shall not die but live, and when I do I will declare the works of the Lord.* Amen.

I shall not die! That's the first thing that the psalm writer says and that really helps us. You know that's a powerful statement: "I shall not die." Not "I don't think I'm going to die"; not "I hope I'm not going to die"; but he says, "I shall not die." Sometimes we say, "I hope I'm not going to die," "I'm keeping my fingers and toes crossed that I don't die," but he says, "I shall not die." The psalmist, who is one of the Jews who have been delivered from captivity, makes a statement of confidence. He makes this statement based on his past that God has already brought him through, and he says with assurance, "I shall not die."

You know, many of us are not even supposed to be here. That's right; some of you sitting in here looking at me now know that you are not supposed to be here. From your birth the odds have been against you. You weren't even supposed to be born; the doctor told your Mama, *you aren't going to carry that baby to term*, and here you are looking at me right now. And when you were small that lady who used to keep you dropped you on your head, or you got hit by a car, or when you were playing in the street you broke your arm, or you fell down the steps—you aren't even supposed to be here because over and over and over the odds have been stacked against you, but here you are. You keep rising again and again and there is something that is within you that says, *I shall not die.*

We have made it against all odds. And we made it because God has been a part of our paths. Even before we even knew, even when we were still in the world, God was with us. We're here because God is a part of our past. God said you will not die but you will live. And because of what God has done in our past we ought to be able to say I shall not die.

If we're going to survive against all odds we have to learn to revisit our past. You know, sometimes we don't like to go back to remember where we've been. It's too painful and sometimes it reminds us that we're not all that. But it's the past that is the key, not only to the present, but sometimes it's the key to the future. The past reminds us that God is good all the time. The past reminds us that God has been with us through thick and thin. The past reminds us that we are a lot tougher than we think. The past reminds us that God bought us a mighty long way.

Has God brought you from a mighty long way? You know, we sing that song . . . *my soul looks back and wonders how I got over.* You know, sometimes when you look back at where you've been and what you've been through, you say I don't even know how I made it. I don't even know how I made it, but we have made it by the grace of God. If we are not afraid to revisit the past, we can find a whole lot to shout about. Some of us are still waiting to find something to shout about, but if you just sit down one day and get quiet by yourself and just think about how God has brought you, you will find yourself getting out of bed and shouting across the floor. When you remember what God has already done, we can find a lot to be thankful for.

We can find a lot of hope and encouragement for what's happening in our lives right now. And the biggest encouragement comes because the past reminds us of the stuff we have gone through. It will remind us that what we went through in the past was much worse than what we are going through right now. I know it seems bad now, but you've been through worse times than this. I know you don't think there were worse times than these, but that's because it's over. It never seems like it was bad when it's over, but if you really think about it you have been through worse times than this. And if we didn't fall apart then, and if we didn't give up then, and if we didn't have a nervous breakdown then, and if we didn't lose our minds then, and if we didn't fold up and die then, then we don't need to do it now. Because when we think about it we've been through a lot worse.

I know it doesn't seem that we've been through worse times, that we've been through worse situations than even now. Don't have any money now? Well, guess what? You've been broke before. How many of you have been broke before? Been so broke that you couldn't even pay attention. Been so broke that you couldn't even find any money in the ashtray. Been so broke you couldn't find money on the dresser. Didn't even have money that you had hid from yourself. I mean broke. But now you're broke and you're wondering how to pay the car note, when before you were broke you didn't even have a car to worry about. You've been broke before. You've been broke before, been sick before, had your credit shot before, when you were afraid to answer the phone. We've had people who walked out on us before. We loved them to death and they walked out on us. We've had these same things happen to us before. We've had friends stab us in the back before. None of this is new. It has happened before and we made it.

And we made it because God was with us. We made it because God didn't leave us nor forsake us. We made it against all odds because God was our refuge and our strength. And because we know what God is like we can say like the psalmist, *I shall not die*. You know sometimes you just have to say to yourself *I shall not die*. You know sometimes it's so rough and it's so bad, but you've got to say to yourself *I shall not die*. It's rough right now but *I shall not die*. Everything seems to be going wrong and against me right now but *I shall not die*. My enemies have joined forces and now are trying to kill me together but *I shall not die*.

I'm going to keep on keeping on; I shall not die. I going to get up from this bed of despair; I shall not die. I'm going to hang in there; I shall not die. I'm not going to give up; I'm not going to turn around; I'm not going to turn God loose; *I shall not die*. Sometimes you've got to say it aloud. Because we've got to learn how to survive against all odds. You know, sometimes it appears as if Satan has released all the demons of hell against you. You ever been there? Sometimes Satan comes himself. We have to learn to say I don't care what goes on; I don't care what's happening; *I shall not die*. Against all odds.

But then the psalmist says a second thing. Not only am I going to say I shall not die but then he says *I will live*. And you know when I first read this passage I said, well, that sounds kind of redundant; that doesn't make any sense. If you are not going to die, then of course you're going to live. Right? Then why would the psalmist say I shall not die but live? And the Spirit said, no, it's not redundant, because it's possible to say in your spirit and to resolve in your spirit that I shall not die but you still haven't gotten the confidence to decide if you're going to live. There are a lot of people who are not dead but they're not living yet either. Amen. Just because you decided you're not going to die, that does not necessarily mean that you've decided that you're going to live. Sometimes we're just existing—no, we're not going to die, and we are going to make it, but we don't have any life, we don't have any joy, we don't have any peace.

Now I don't know about you, but that's not living. That's not living. It's possible to just exist. And if we're really going to make it against all odds, not only must we make up our minds to not die, but we must also make up our minds to live. It's not living to be in a constant state of fear; that's not living. It's not living to be in a constant state of frustration; that's not living. It's not living to be in a constant state of anger and animosity all the time; that's not living. And God wants us to live. Jesus said, *I have come that you might have life and have it more abundantly. I have come that you won't be sitting on the side of the bed every morning trying to get yourself together before you can even go out and face the day. That's not living. I have come that you might have life and have it more abundantly.*

If we're going to live we must surround ourselves with positive people. You know, oftentimes we cannot live because we are hanging with people who are about death. We're hanging around people who are busy making funeral arrangements. And so while we're crying they're busy telling us, *"You're right; you're not going to make it. Yes, it is bad; oh yes, I don't know how you're going to make it either."* They're about the business of making funeral arrangements. But if we're going to live we have to surround ourselves with positive people.

Do you remember when Jesus was going to heal Dorcus? When he got to the house to heal Dorcus, all these women were in the room and they were crying, *Oh poor Dorcus.* They were prepared to fix her up for the funeral. And Jesus had to ask all of them to get out because he was going to heal her and bring her back to life. Sometimes you have put those people who are about death out of your life because Jesus wants to heal you and bring you back to life. We all have to put those death people out of our path because Jesus wants to bring us back to life. We have to surround ourselves with people who are positive. If you fool around with people who have nothing to lose, then eventually they will see to it that you will lose everything. Did you know that? A lot of times we are fooling around with people who have nothing to lose so they can afford to be negative; they have nothing to lose. They can afford to be as negative as they want to be. The people who have no spouse are always the ones who tell you to put your spouse out. Think about it, they have nothing to lose, but if you fool around with them you'll lose everything you have.

People who don't have any money are always the ones to tell you how to spend your money. Well, they don't have anything to lose, and you fool around with them and you end up without a dime. Well, they didn't have a dime to begin with in the first place. We have to hang around with positive people, people who are moving forward and are not content to live in the past, people who when you feel like giving up are going to come and encourage you, give you a word of encouragement, and want to pull you forward, and when you say *I think I can* they say *Of course you can*. We need people who when you say *I'm going to try* they push you on, getting behind you and pushing you on, getting in front of you and pulling you; people who will allow you to cry on their shoulder but will say *Alright now, it's time to stop crying; let's get up and get busy*. Positive people. If you're going to make it against all odds then you need positive people in your life.

And then if we're going to live we also have to stop being so passive. I have never seen so many passive black people in my life. You know we are watching *Roots* every Saturday, and if we were back there in the time of *Roots* we would have just folded up and died. The first time somebody talked about chopping a toe off . . . We can't get a lot if we're going to be passive. And the Lord Jesus Christ whom we serve was not a passive Lord. People don't want to kill passive people. If Jesus had been as passive as they wanted him to be they never would have killed him at age 33. Because when you're passive you don't make any waves. When you're passive you don't ever bother anybody, you don't upset any system. If Jesus was as passive as we make him out to be then he would not have died on a cross; he would have lived to be 90 years old rocking in a chair somewhere. And nobody would have bothered him, nobody would have messed with him, and by the same token you and I would have never been saved.

Stop being so passive. You know, we tolerate anything as Christians. We come to church, and we shout and everything, and we know that when we go home we have one room we can be in, and we can't even come out of that room, and we're watching a little 13-inch black-and-white TV, and we can't even come out to tell the children to cut the TV down, to cut the stereo down. We are too passive. We let people come into our homes and take over our neighborhoods and do anything. We are too passive. And if we're going to survive against all odds we have stop being passive and say to ourselves and to our enemies and to Satan, "No, I'm going to live. I'm going to get up here and I'm going to live. I'm going to smile again, I'm going to have joy again, I'm going to have peace again. I'm going to live."

If we're going to live, we must realize also that we have everything that we need. You know, sometimes we want to live and we're still waiting for God to give us something. We have everything we need. Say we have everything we need. You have everything that you need. What you have is what you need. If you don't have it you don't need it. What you have is what you need.

Now when you dare to use what you need, which you already have, maybe God will give you something else. We want something else. Just like David—he used a slingshot. If he had waited for a 99 whatever . . . but God said you don't need that; a slingshot will do. You have what you need. Whatever you have will do. Don't worry about how small it is; whatever you have it will do if you trust God with it. You have what you need.

We say God is a present help in time of trouble. I don't think we always understand that. What that means is that today is the tomorrow we were worried about last week. Think about that. Today is the tomorrow we used to worry about. We used to sit up all night long to worry about it, but it is here and God has supplied for our needs. He has been our present help, and when we get to the future God will be there. He will be our present help in time of trouble. We have to understand that we have everything we need. We can live.

I don't know about you, but not only am I going to not die but I've decided to live today. Have you decided to really live today no matter what the odds are? Have you decided that you're going to live no matter what you have to face? Have you decided that you're going to live with God, that you're going to live no matter what, in spite of, because God has said so? Have you decided that you are going to live? You know, nobody else can decide that but you. The psalmist didn't say to the people you shall not die; he said that I shall not die but live. Everybody has to claim and own it for themselves. And until you decide your Mama can come and help you, and your Daddy can help you, and you can have a good man, and you can have a good job—until you decide that you are going to live you're not going to live. Today you have to rise up and say I shall not die but live.

And then the last part of this text as I close is that it's not just about not dying and living but it's also about "And declare the works of the Lord." In other words, all this is for a reason, so we might declare the works of the Lord. During the time of the psalmist the plight of the worshipper paid an important part in worship. When a person came to worship, whatever their plight was, if they were going through something or things were going well for them, it determined how powerful their God was, how powerful the God they served was. If you went out to battle and you did not win the battle then they would say you must not serve a powerful God because your God allowed you not to have the victory. But if you went out and you were victorious and you defeated your enemy and you had food and shelter and all that you needed, then the people wouldn't say "you," but they would say whatever God you were serving, that God must be a mighty powerful God. The psalmist must have understood that because throughout Israel's history they were always quick to point out that they served Jehovah God who was a deliverer, a way maker, a source of strength, a healer, and a deliverer.

The psalmist was quick to point out that now that they are back home and free from captivity in Babylon, they would now be able to declare the works of the Lord. They would now become a source of witness and testimony to the power and the strength of their God. Now when people see them they will know without a shadow of doubt that their God is the only true and living God. The psalmist knows that the deliverance was not just for them, not to give them bragging rights, but to give them the opportunity to show forth the glory and the honor to their God. And nonbelievers might know that Jehovah God is a supreme ruler of heaven and earth.

And that's the way it is with us too. Once we purpose in our hearts to not die but to live we become a testimony to the power of almighty God. And whenever we make it against all odds, we ought to have a testimony. We ought to be willing to endure and come through the test and be able to have a testimony. You know, sometimes people don't want to give their testimony and I always say no matter how small they are, it's not about you—it's about God. Because you want people to know that God works in big things and God works in small things too. When people stand at this mic and give their testimony, it's not about them; it's not about them wanting to stand up here being seen; it's about showing forth what God has done, that God might get the glory and God might get the praise.

Before you can have a testimony you have to be willing to go through the test. Look at the word testimony and you see the word "test." That's the bulk of it—test. But see, we want the "mony" without the test. We don't want to go through the test. If you want a testimony it means that you have been willing to go through the test. But it's more than having a testimony—we become the testimony. When God brings you through against all odds, it gives glory to God that your God has delivered you, that your God has sustained you, that your God did not allow you to perish.

Every time people see you, they ought to start shouting, because they were there, they saw you when the doctor said, I don't think she'll make it through the night. When people see you they ought to shout because they saw you when you were wrapped up in sin and didn't even know you were in the world, and now they see you talking about God. They ought to start shouting, *That's a good God!* We become a testimony. We can declare the works of the Lord. We can declare that the God whom we serve is a God who is faithful; that the God whom we serve will bring you up when you're down real low; that the God whom we serve will forgive you; that the God whom we serve will give you a second chance; that the God whom we serve will bless your life over and over and over again. We are a testimony not to ourselves but to the might and the power and the grace of almighty God. We should be able to declare the works of the Lord.

This is an exciting text. We can get so bogged down and so depressed, with Satan robbing us of our joy and making us feel defeated every day, but we have to begin to rise up in our spirit, with that little mustard seed of faith, and look Satan straight in the face and say, You are a liar; I shall not die but I will live. You know, sometimes Satan does get you; sometimes you just have to say to Satan, You got me today but I shall not die, I will live, because I have tomorrow, and God is going to be in the tomorrow, and I am going to get up. I'm not going to stay down there. I may be down for the count this time, but I'm not going to stay down. I'm going to get up and I'm going to walk with God. I shall not die; I'm going to live.

As I close I want to share a little something for you to always remember. They say that lions are the king of the jungle, but when they get real old they lose their teeth. So the old lions have no teeth but they have a ferocious roar. That's that roar that we have come to know when we watch the MGM movies. It's the young lions in their prime that have the teeth that are so sharp that they can rip you apart. And so when they go out on hunting expeditions, the old seasoned lions get at one end of the forest and the young lions get at the other, and all the old lions do is roar; they just roar. And if you are the prey, when you hear the roar of these old lions you run away from them, but you run right into the jaws of these young, strong lions. And so we need to remember what some of the smarter animals of the jungle know: when you hear the roar don't run away from the roar—run toward the roar.

In life you've got to learn to run toward the roar, because by the time you get there God has taken the teeth out of the situation. By the time you get there God has locked the jaws of the lion and you shall survive. I don't know about you, but how many of you have survived against all odds? Did somebody give up on you, yet you survived against all odds? Has God made a way? Has God brought you out? Has God blessed you? Has God changed your life? Well, you ought to stand on your feet and give God the glory. He is a mighty, mighty good God. He's a marvelous God. He's a glorious God.

We thank you, God, that you didn't let us perish. We thank you, God, that you didn't let us die. I'm running toward the roar—toward the roar of sickness—toward the roar of trials and tribulations—toward the roar of death and destruction. I don't know about you, but by the grace of God, I shall not die; I'm going to live . . .

A Mother's Love

THERE IS ABSOLUTELY NOTHING LIKE A MOTHER'S LOVE. A mother's love is soothing and keeps us steadfast and sure as a woman. A mother's love guides and shapes how we approach life. Without the love of a strong mother, we never know how special we are and how powerful we are. A mother's love shapes all that we do or don't do as a woman: who we will love, how we will love, or even if we are capable of loving at all.

I have a wonderful, loving mother. There are so many stories that speak of her unconditional love through the years. My mother's love has always been constant. When I was a little girl, she was waiting when I arrived home from school. Through the years, she was behind every project, everything I desired to do. My mother's love caused me to dream big, to believe that I could do more and be more than anything I had seen others do or be. My mother's love has been amazing. My mother has been the quiet strength beneath my wings—she pushes, she lifts, she is the master encourager.

My mother's love has been my source of strength during my illness. When I woke up from surgery and saw that they had brought her down to the hospital and she was sitting quietly in a chair beside my bed, it blessed my soul. I felt the comfort I had come to know throughout my lifetime. I knew that if *Mama* is here, everything will be alright. I could tell that she was not fully aware of all that was going on, but she seemed to sense that it was a hospital room and her baby girl needed her to be there. She gently reached out and rubbed my face and simply asked, *Are you okay?* She was in second-stage dementia but she was ever the mother, ever the caregiver.

I am grateful for the love of my earthy mother, that wonderful, caring woman who loves me unconditionally and desires the very best for me. But I am always mindful that Mother God is my eternal source of strength. As I walk through this journey, Mother God draws me close, and holds me in her arms, and kisses me gently. She is ever-present to soothe me through the painful days and the restless nights. Mother God keeps me encouraged and whispers words of hope to my spirit when I feel like giving up. I love her and I know with an assurance that she loves me!

Dear Mother God, thank you for your loving care! Thank you for being that gentle Spirit who abides with us always. Your presence comforts us and keeps us hopeful. Mother God, thank you for your unconditional love. Amen.

Being a Patient

I AM NOT A GOOD PATIENT. I am a terrible patient. I'm sure my husband and closest family members would agree. I don't like to follow orders. I don't like to take medicine. I don't like to keep doctors' appointment. But cancer does not have room or time for persons who refuse to be good patients. To be or not to be a good patient is not an option when you have cancer. Your life is literally on the line. So reluctantly and with a great deal of inward grumbling, I consented to be a patient in order that I could get well. But there were many times when being a patient was a pain.

As a patient, you are no longer in control. You are given direction and orders, and, for the most part, they are not to be questioned. As a patient you have to wait. The doctor does not belong to you alone; there are others ahead of you. As a patient you have to give people the same information over and over again, every time they see you, as if they're seeing you for the first time. As a patient you have to do what you are told when you are told and the way you are told. I'm not used to being a patient.

As a patient, I had to trust people I did not know. I had to be confident in the knowledge and skills of people based solely on their job position and their title. I had to believe in medicine and procedures that didn't make me feel better although I was told that they were healing me. I was not a good patient. I wanted to know and to be in charge and to control and to direct. And I was not allowed to do any of that.

Every cancer patient is unique. Every cancer patient expects to be healed and believes that the answer to their progress is found in what they personally do to get well. So it is very difficult to do what we are told to do if it we see no results. Following the process is difficult for us. But, thank God, there are those who are willing to help us to be the patients we need to be. Thank God for the doctors and nurses who put up with our endless questions, our constant whining over routine things, and our occasional bouts of bad behavior. It's crucial that I be a good patient so I can get well.

Being a patient is what I am called to be at this time in my life. I have to accept that. I have to be alright with that. I have to be quiet and listen. I have to allow others to help me. I have to be obedient. I know this in my head, now I have to know it in my heart. Being a patient is a necessity and a blessing.

Dear Lord, we confess that we have not always been good patients. Forgive us for our impatience with the progress of our treatment. Thank you for the patience of our doctors and nurses. Help us to be the patients that our caregivers need us to be. We put our healing process in your hands. Amen.

Another Birthday

I'M GETTING READY TO CELEBRATE ANOTHER BIRTHDAY. That means a year has almost passed since I was diagnosed with cancer. This is a milestone. This is exciting and worthy of celebration. But like most cancer patients, I don't want to celebrate too much, too prematurely. I don't want to celebrate as if this is the last birthday I'm going to have. Yet, as always, this is in the back of my mind. But hallelujah, I made it to another birthday!

Birthdays have always been special in our family. Birthdays never go uncelebrated. Birthdays are a rallying point for family and friends to let you know how much they love and care for you. This birthday was no different except for the fact that I have cancer. How do you spend your birthday when you have cancer? Do you do something big or spend a quiet evening with close friends? As I pondered how I wanted to spend my birthday, I was keenly aware that the wheels were working with my family and friends. My birthday was on a weekday, Tuesday Bible Study Night. This allowed me to have the day free. I chose to spend the day with my mother. I chose to sit with her and to gather strength from her as her only daughter and firstborn. Even with dementia, her presence gave me a great deal of strength.

My family and friends were awesome. They showered me with cards, flowers, and gifts. They wanted so much for this birthday to be something special. I had mixed emotions, happy and sad at the same time. I needed to slip away for some quiet time by myself to process how I should feel. I remember God speaking to me in those quiet moments, reminding me that however I felt was okay. God reminded me that cancer does not come with a playbook, that there is no right or wrong way. I am grieving the loss of life as I knew it before cancer and there is no script for me to follow. This is not just another birthday; on this birthday, I am in the fight of my life and that fact cannot be ignored.

God was gracious on this 56th birthday. I felt blessed to be in the land of the living. I felt encouraged to serve a God who does not always give us what we desire but is always mindful and attentive to what we need. So on this birthday, God reassured me that I am loved abundantly; I am God's special child, and God is healing me. For that I am grateful.

Dear Lord, thank you for keeping us to see another birthday. You have spared us and we are grateful for your healing power. May this birthday remind us that you have created us to fulfill a divine purpose in this life. Let us live with expectation each and every day. Amen.

Barry Died!

MY FRIEND BARRY DIED. During the course of my illness, my friend Barry died. It was devastating. I was crushed. When Barry received his diagnosis, I was through chemo, surgery, and radiation. I was feeling good about my chances for survival. And because God had been gracious to me, I had no doubt that Barry would survive as well. But Barry died!

I had become the poster child among ministers with regard to cancer. Whenever anyone they knew was diagnosed with cancer, they were instructed to call Pat. I remember my initial conversations with Barry. I shared what I knew about the disease and its treatment, being careful to caution him that, while similar, everyone's journey is different. I prayed with him and reassured him that he could endure all that lay ahead. I had started my journal and I e-mailed him some entries to encourage him. I urged him to begin his own journal so that he would have a written record of what God was going to do in his life.

When I heard that he was out of the pulpit, I thought it was temporary while he underwent his treatments. Then his wife shared that they were seeking a cancer treatment center that offered more aggressive treatment than he had been receiving. I continued to pray, confident that God was indeed healing my friend Barry. Then I heard that he was in the hospital and it didn't look good. And while I paused to wrap my mind around that fact and get myself together to visit, Barry died.

I remember sitting in my study and crying like a baby. Why Barry? All I could think of was his wonderful wife of over 25 years, his beautiful daughter who was only a few years older than my daughter, and the wonderful congregation he had led for over 15 years. Why Barry? I felt guilty. Why not me? I wanted Barry to live. I had told Barry he would make it. I wanted to scream: *God, how can you do this? I told Barry he would be alright!* I felt that God had personally let ME down. I felt that God had forsaken ME. I felt worse about Barry's death than about my own diagnosis and prognosis.

As always, God was patient with me. God let me rant and rave about what I felt should have happened. And then, as I sat alone in my office, God reminded me that both life and death are God's business, under God's control. God reminded me that each of us is unique and God deals with us according to God's perfect will for us. God reminded me that this had nothing to do with what God was doing in my life. God reminded me that healing is still God's business.

As I visited his wife and daughter, I was sad but was made glad as we reminisced about the wonderful person Barry was. His legacy of care and love for people is ours to live into. I am still comforted by that easy smile and joyful laugh that filled every space he was. I thank God for allowing him to touch the life of me and my family. I wanted healing on this side but I humbly submit to the divine will of God, and I rejoice in the fact that now Barry has been healed.

Dear Lord, thank you for being God over both life and death. Help us to receive your healing, no matter how it comes. We pray for peace in whatever your will is for our lives. Lord, we will not fear, but we will put our trust in you. Amen.

Being Loved Again

I HAD AVOIDED IT. My husband had walked with me every step of the way during my diagnosis, chemo, surgery, and radiation. He had been there when I was too sick to lift my head off the pillow after the chemo sessions. He was there to encourage me during those dark days after surgery. But I found myself dreading the time when we would return to lovemaking. So I avoided it by focusing on my illness both day and night. He was patient but I knew that the time would come when we would have to face this hurdle as we had crossed the others.

There was no plan. One day I came home and as we sat quietly together enjoying one another's company without talking, a spirit of intense longing engulfed both of us. I immediately recognized our unspoken signals of the past, but secretly I was terrified because I had refused to allow my husband to really focus on my body since the surgery. I usually dressed in the dressing room adjacent to our private bathroom and I did so quickly. I jumped into bed at night and immediately pretended to go to sleep. I didn't know how to get back into the routine of our lovemaking. Although I knew he loved me, I was afraid that he would be repulsed by my body. I remember letting out a sigh as if to allow myself to submit to the moment and to allow God to guide us through it.

As my husband took me by the hand and gently led me back to the bedroom, I asked God to be in the midst of all that would happen. Our lovemaking was a spectacular spiritual happening. God was indeed with us. My husband's every touch was reassuring and affirming that he loved me and that he loved my body. I was moved to tears at his lack of hesitation to touch and kiss the place where my breast had once been. As my husband and I renewed our intimacy with one another, I realized the awesome gift of lovemaking between those who are in covenant relationship with one another. I became a virgin again, giving the essence of my womanhood to a man who loves me and whose love for me inspires and excites me.

On that day, God was marvelously present and reminded us what we had come to know during the eighteen years of our marriage: God is with us always—with us in the living room, with us in the family room, and with us in our bedroom. And whenever God blesses us, we find ourselves praising God and saying, Hallelujah!

Dear Lord, thank you for making us spiritual and sexual beings. Thank you for the gift of sexual intimacy between married couples. Help us, Lord, to turn even this aspect of our lives over to you that you might bless us as we bless one another. Amen.

It's Not Over

JUST WHEN I THOUGHT I WAS ON MY WAY, THERE'S SOMETHING ELSE TO CONTEND WITH. My mother-in-law, a twenty-year breast cancer survivor, has lymphedema. Her right arm on the side where she underwent her mastectomy is considerably larger than her left. This condition is a common occurrence for cancer patients. After a while, the blood to the missing beast is redirected and fluid begins to build up in the arm. Once I was diagnosed with cancer and underwent a mastectomy, I prayed that I would not develop lymphedema.

Within six months of completing my radiation treatment, I began to see signs of lymphedema. I noticed a slight increase in the size of my right upper arm in comparison to my left arm. When I told my oncologist, she immediately measured both arms. Yes, there was a significant difference in size. She immediately sent me to a massage therapist who would help me learn to massage my right side and redirect the flow of blood to decrease the build-up of fluid. In addition I was given a girdle type of garment to wear on my right arm to restrict the swelling and to keep my arm from swelling further. I was devastated because I thought I was out of the woods, but it's not over.

Lymphedema is often seen as a natural byproduct of breast cancer. In fact, twenty years earlier, my mother-in-law was told to prepare for it because there was nothing that could be done. Therefore, she had learned to live with the enlarged arm and the numbness associated with it. Since that time, many strides have been made. The massage therapy was a new approach and was getting good results among patients. While it could not reverse the swelling, it could halt the swelling and prevent it from advancing.

Massage therapy was new to me. Massage therapy is different from the massages I had received at spas. Massage therapy involves gentle stroking, not pressure or kneading. It is much more intimate and personal. My massage therapist was marvelous, but I had to learn to trust her. It was uncomfortable to allow her to touch my body and stroke my arm and left side to redirect the flow of blood. But eventually, I learned to tolerate it and even look forward to that hour of soothing, gentle massage. I was taught to self-massage so that once the therapist was done, I could continue the treatment myself. Also, the therapist held two sessions with my husband to teach him how to do the massages so he could do that for me at home. Those sessions were wonderful for us as a couple.

It's not over. In this life it's rarely ever over. There is always something else to contend with. Cancer is no different. There is always something else, always something unexpected, an unforeseen occurrence. But we can find comfort in knowing that God is with us, ever-present to deal with what we did not see coming and what we cannot handle alone.

Dear Lord, this journey has been very frustrating. It seems to never be done; there's always something more standing in our path. Lord, give us the strength to endure the next obstacle, the next hurdle. With you on our side, we know we will make it. Amen.

Anticlimactic

I HAD LOOKED FORWARD TO THIS DAY. My treatment is finally over. I'm technically a cancer survivor now. I've survived two rounds of intense chemotherapy. I've survived a mastectomy. I've survived weeks of radiation. I've survived massage therapy for lymphedema. I've survived constant appointments with the surgeon, the oncologist, and the radiologist. I've survived the pain, the uncertainty, the loss of my hair, and the loss of my mobility. And now, I am told very calmly as I go for a routine visit that my treatment is complete. I will only need to see my doctors yearly. I thought I would shout on this day. I thought I would be overjoyed on this day. But after all I've been through the news is, at best, anticlimactic.

Sometimes the anticipation of something is climactic. Every piece of my journey had its own built-in climax. Getting through the surgery was climactic. Finishing the first round of chemotherapy was climactic. Finishing the second round of chemotherapy was climactic. Completing the radiation session was climactic. All along the way, there had been enormous peaks that called for celebration. So it was quite anticlimactic to be told that finally my treatments were over.

I remember sitting quietly after receiving the news. My doctor had to ask me if I was alright. She explained that my reaction was common for cancer patients. My thoughts were: *Is this it? Where are the fireworks? Why do I feel let down? What is wrong with me; shouldn't I feel happier?* It's hard to describe the feeling I experienced on moving from treatment to maintenance. In a way, I felt abandoned. Now I'm on my own, without the constant care of doctors, no longer under the watchful eyes of those who have cared for me during this process. I felt a little lost.

The end to my treatments sent me into a slight state of depression. And I couldn't tell anyone. How do you tell people that you're depressed because your cancer treatments are over? How do you explain to people why you don't feel overjoyed? When I relayed the news to my husband, he immediately picked up on the fact that I was less than thrilled. He helped me to understand that what I was feeling was fear, fear of the unknown.

For the cancer patient, once treatment is over signals a return to ground zero. Our cancer is now free to return. It signals that we no longer have the covering of a medical team who translates every symptom, ache, and pain. Now we have to acknowledge anew that God is in control. When my treatment was over, I didn't feel like rejoicing because I was not sure rejoicing was in order. I simply felt enormously blessed and once again I felt hopeful that God would be ever-faithful.

Dear Lord, thank you for allowing us to reach this milestone. No more treatments. Now we move forward to total healing. Calm our doubts and fears. Just as we have trusted you throughout this process, help us to trust you now. Heal our bodies. Amen.

Daring to Grieve

GRIEF COMES WHENEVER WE LOSE SOMEONE OR SOMETHING WE LOVE. We grieve the loss of loved ones, but we also grieve the loss of jobs and relationships. And every cancer patient has to eventually grieve the loss of our life before cancer. It takes a while but we will have to grieve. Grief is one of those emotions that says, *either you pay me now or you pay me later*. When we ignore our grief, it bottles up and can do some irreversible damage in the future. We have to dare to grieve.

It took me a while. I was afraid to give in to my grief. I was afraid to admit that I was grieving who I used to be before I was diagnosed with cancer. I was silent and tried to pretend that nothing had changed. I tried to encourage everyone else, but I was ignoring my own feelings of loss. I had to give myself permission to grieve. I had to dare to grieve.

When you're sick, grieving for yourself is complicated. There is a thin line between expressing legitimate grief and wallowing in self-pity. I didn't want to find myself doing the latter. I knew that when people wallow in their own self-pity, it can be a turn-off and it turns self-destructive very quickly. As a pastor, there were people still depending on me to be a strong shepherd who could be a model for them in dealing with their own grief and suffering. How do I find the balance? How do I dare to grieve?

I had become accustomed to managing my grief by giving constant updates on my health. These updates were given freely and instantly so that I would not have to deal with my own feelings. But grief can be ignored only for so long. Eventually your grief gets in the way of everything you're doing. Your grief wakes you up at night and your grief taps you on the shoulder and is the silent partner in every conversation. It settles in your eyes and you find that it has to get out somehow. I had to dare to grieve.

I found that when I dared to grieve for myself that I found God in the midst of my grief. The day that I sat down and cried for all the lost things that could never be, God revealed all the things that God could still make possible. When I dared to grieve, I also dared to give every feeling to God and trust that God could handle them. When I dared to grieve, I found out that I didn't need to shoulder everything inside of myself. When I dared to have my moments, I discovered that it was alright to have fears and doubts and to not be strong because I serve a mighty God who has all power. When I dared to grieve, I discovered God anew and I began once again to allow God to be in control.

Dear Lord, I'm grieving right now. I feel the loss of life as I once knew it. I sometimes feel as if nothing will ever be the same. But I know that you are always the same. So Lord, help me to deal with the changes in my life. Help me to let go and to move forward with you as my guide. I need you, Lord. Amen.

Accepting the Changes

AT SOME POINT IN TIME, WE HAVE TO ACCEPT THE CHANGES THAT CANCER HAS BROUGHT INTO OUR LIVES. There are many physical changes, but there are also emotional changes as well. After cancer, we are never the same. As a woman, it was sometimes difficult to accept the changes. Sometimes I struggled with the changes. But eventually I set myself on the path of accepting the changes in my life.

Some of the changes were hard, like the loss of hair and the loss of mobility. I was one of only four of my doctor's patients whose hair did not grow back. I had to deal with that. It became my symbolic look, a bald head in a day of abundant, beautiful hair. But I chose to accept my reality and sport this increasingly popular bald look. It did not take me long to accept the changes in my looks. Of all the changes, these were probably the easiest to accept.

I still struggle with accepting the changes in my mobility. I want to be able to walk without pain again. I want to be able to run and move swiftly again. I want to not be dependent upon a cane, a walker, a mobile chair. These changes are hard to accept. But I am blessed to be able to drive and to move to the extent that I can. I'm accepting that this is my reality now.

The mental changes are subtle. I forget names more often. I tire more easily. I have to endure periods when I find it hard to concentrate. There are some changes that this disease has forced me to accept. It's sometimes hard to distinguish between which are due to the cancer and which are due to old age. But it does not really matter; life is different now and I have to accept that.

Cancer forces us to deal with change. We all know that but we avoid dealing with change if we can. But cancer forces us to deal with change. With cancer, changes cannot and will not be ignored or go undealt with. So I have to deal with how I look, how I move, what I can do, what I can no longer do, and how I feel. I've found this to be a blessing. God has taught me that change is the gateway to growth and new possibilities. God has taught me that change does not close doors; change opens doors. I have been challenged to accept the changes in my life, but I'm grateful for them. I have discovered that God is in the changes, and with each new change, God ushers in new possibilities.

Dear Lord, help us to accept the changes in our lives. Help us to deal with this new reality that cancer has brought. We need you to be with us as we struggle to maintain life as we have come to know it. Even though things change, you remain faithful to us in all things. Amen.

Preaching through the Storm

I MISSED ONLY ONE SUNDAY FROM THE PULPIT DURING MY ILLNESS. That was by God's grace. God allowed me to preach through the storm of cancer. In fact, the preaching was a part of my healing balm. The Word healed me as it went forth to heal others in the body. Preaching was therapeutic. I have always relied on the Holy Spirit to be with me in the preaching moment, but during my illness I became more keenly aware of the presence of God's Holy Spirit as I preached. I was more aware that I was only a vessel in the enterprise of preaching. Preaching, which had always been a sacred moment for me, became an even more sacred moment. It was as if I was outside of my body, expending strength and energy I did not have. I left the preaching moment drained but also strangely refreshed and renewed. God was gracious to give me the strength to preach through the storm.

I have never considered myself to be a great preacher. I am a lectionary preacher who is diligent to do the exegesis to relate God's Word to the concerns of people in this present age. I see myself as a messenger, letting the people know *thus saith the Lord*. During my illness, my health and physical strength did not always allow my usual preparation time. Even though I had asked to do my chemo early in the week to allow me to be well enough to preach by the weekend, that did not always happen. There were many weeks when I arrived at church weak and nauseated prior to preaching. Sometimes I had to leave the pulpit to go to my study for a moment before preaching. But God was gracious to use me to bless the people and to deliver a Word that was relevant and spoke to the needs of the people.

When I was a young preacher, I had read Dr. Beecher Hicks's book *Preaching through a Storm*, but I had no idea what that meant. As I read it, I sensed that the storm Dr. Hicks was talking about was unrest in the church. But my storm was personal illness. I was preaching to people who loved me but who needed a Word to get them through the week. Although they loved me, they needed a strong pastor who could preach with strength and conviction. I had to rely on God to see me through. I did not want my physical health to be the focus of the preaching moment. I prayed that God would allow the Word to come through strong in spite of the weakness of the vessel delivering it.

By the grace of Almighty God, I learned to preach through my storm. People came to know the Lord during this season of preaching. People were strengthened during this season of preaching. And preaching made me stronger physically. I would arrive at church weak, but at the preaching moment God was in full control and gave me supernatural, divine strength and power. And the preaching healed and blessed me. I did not die but I became stronger by the power of God's healing Word to both the preacher and the waiting pew.

Dear Lord, thank you for your Word that heals and meets us at the point of all our needs. Bless all preachers and pastors who must stand and preach in spite of their own personal storms. Lord, give us the strength to do all of those things you have called us do. Give us your divine power. Amen.

My Daddy's Strength

MY DADDY WAS A STRONG, QUIET MAN. As a child, I thought he was the tallest, most powerful man in the world. His quiet, strong presence made us feel safe and cared for. When Daddy came home, we rejoiced. He represented stability, and with him around we felt that no hurt, harm, and danger could touch us. My Daddy was strong and he was my protector. His strength was reassuring. My Daddy died two years before I was diagnosed with cancer, but his strength continues to walk with me each and every day. My Daddy's strength was never more present than during my cancer journey.

Everyone in my family knows that I am a Daddy's girl. Everyone in my family know that my Daddy and I were close and had a special bond. My Daddy and I would spend hours together, just sitting, enjoying one another's company and presence. We didn't have to do a lot of talking. Just being with my Daddy was sufficient. He had a way of reassuring you without speaking a word. His gentle eyes and soft words made you feel as if you could do anything, be anything, get through anything.

When I was diagnosed with cancer, I really missed my Daddy's physical presence. I longed for those quiet moments on the porch and those gentle reflective talks. I missed his wisdom, his fatherly love and protection. I missed my Daddy. But I soon found that my Daddy's strength was being miraculously poured into me on a daily basis.

I had heard that whenever you find a shiny new penny, it means that a departed loved one is watching over you. Immediately after my Daddy died, I had found such a shiny penny here and there, and when I did it gave me great joy. But once I was diagnosed with cancer, the pennies began to appear almost on a daily basis, and always when I desperately needed extra reassurance. My Daddy's strength was ever-present. My Daddy spoke to my spirit at my lowest moments. My Daddy would come up in my spirit when I felt weak and when I was unsure.

A Daddy's love and strength is amazing. My Daddy was no longer physically present but he still was available when I needed him. And while my Daddy's strength was available to inspire me to not give up, his spirit also served to remind me that I am blessed to have a Heavenly Father who will never leave me nor forsake me. It is my heavenly Father who is my ultimate power source and who is available to heal me day by day.

Dear Lord, we thank you for the love and strength of our earthly fathers and mothers. We thank you for their strength that comforts us in our time of need. Heavenly Mother and Father, thank you for loving us unconditionally and for being ever-present in our lives. Amen.

Living without Fear

FEAR IS A PERSISTENT EMOTION. Fear can stay with you. Fear can walk with you. Fear can live with you night and day. And for most people with cancer, fear is something that we learn to live with. We wake up daily and begin our journey with fear. We are afraid of the disease. We are afraid of what the disease may do to our bodies. We are afraid of what cancer can do. We are afraid of the cancer spreading. And even when the disease is under control, we are afraid of the cancer returning. Fear becomes a way of life and we look forward to living without fear.

I don't know when fear became a constant companion. It started as a slight pause when people would ask me how I was doing. It graduated to an uncomfortable feeling in the pit of my stomach before each doctor's visit. It finally hid behind a smile and a friendly greeting. No one knew how afraid I was. No one knew I was living with fear each and every day.

Living without fear was one of my biggest challenges. Living without fear involves living a life that sees and embraces more than my cancer. Living without fear is moving forward and daring to expect a future without cancer. All cancer survivors have to learn to live without fear. Fear can be conquered. And it has to be conquered in our mind because the mind has to be reconditioned to see things without prejudice. Fear pre-judges everything. Fear weighs everything from the time-frame of before and after cancer. And everything that we cannot connect to as pre- or post-cancer causes us to fear. There appears to be no in-between ground.

I cannot count the times that God brought to my remembrance the scripture that declares: *God does not give us a spirit of fear.* And to be sure, fear is a spirit that does not match well with God's spirit of peace and freedom from anxiety. I had to decide which spirit I would allow to dwell in me and which spirit I would allow to walk with me during this journey. I had to learn to live without fear.

It was a slow walk back down the path I had come. I had to live without fear in my mind and then in my words and finally in my actions. Living without fear came as I dared to give the fear to a God who reminded me that I could trust God to do what seemed impossible. On a daily basis I had to walk by faith, getting up and facing the unknown journey called life without any guarantee except God's promise to be with me. With each tiny step, I found myself shedding the fear; and gradually I found myself living without fear. It was God's doing.

Dear Lord, you are not the author of fear. As we deal with the fears of this life, we need you to free us to live a joy-filled and peaceful life without fear. Amen.

A Sense of Humor

YOU CAN'T ENDURE THIS CANCER JOURNEY WITHOUT A SENSE OF HUMOR. You have to be able to laugh—at yourself, at your situation, and at what you're going through. Laughter is therapeutic for the body and the soul. At first, it's hard to laugh, hard to find anything funny. But after you realize that the disease is not going away anytime soon, you go back and reclaim your sense of humor because you realize you're going to need it. As a cancer patient, you learn how to laugh and how to laugh often. It beats crying.

I have always loved to laugh and I had to reclaim my sense of humor. At first, people didn't know if it was okay to laugh around me. Things were so serious. People talked in low voices. They had solemn looks on their faces. They looked sad and they sounded sad. They wanted to relegate my conversations to serious religious matters about life and death and prayer and divine healing. But there were times when I just wanted to laugh. My sense of humor found something to be funny. I joked about my lack of hair and my inability to shout anymore. I joked about not being able to chase my husband around the house any longer. At first, people were afraid to joke with me. They felt they were being disrespectful. But I refused to give up my sense of humor. What was funny before cancer was still funny now.

I had to balance the seriousness of what was going on with my body with humor. I watched all of my favorite comedies. My friends gave me videos of my favorite comedians. The church members gave me a basket of joke books and people even called to tell me their favorite jokes—*have you heard the one about . . .* I laughed and laughed. It was, as the Bible says, like medicine to my soul. One night we had "joke night" at church where members had to tell clean jokes to make Pastor (me) laugh. What a blessing it was.

God blesses us with the gift of laughter. No matter what we have to go through, laughter will make you feel better. I chose to laugh my way through what I had to deal with. I was blessed to have doctors and caregivers who had a great sense of humor, and they kept me up in spite of the challenges we faced. God has a sense of humor and God shares that sense of humor with us. I have felt God's laughter when I needed it most. It's God's laughter that has kept me alive until this present moment.

Dear Lord, thank you for the gift of laughter. Thank you for the moments when we find something that brings us joy in spite of what we're going through. Lord, continue to give us a sense of humor and dispel all of our sadness. Amen.

As Normal as It Gets

IT'S AS NORMAL AS IT GETS. It was hard getting to that point, the point of realizing that things were as normal as they were going to get. Now it is normal to accept the fact that you are disabled. Now it is normal to live with some type of pain. Now it is normal to have good days as well as "bad" days. Now daily naps and pillboxes full of pills are normal. Now it's normal to feel anxious and to feel uncomfortable when I go to the doctor. I have to get used to this new normal that causes me to feel vulnerable. With all of its ups and downs, this is as normal as it gets.

Normal is relative. Normal is based on what used to be normal and what you have come to know as normal. Normal for me was being a high-energy, healthy, sharp, and self-reliant woman. This prior understanding of normal had allowed me to wear many hats. This normal had allowed me to be involved in many things at the same time. This normal had allowed me to work at an unbelievable pace and do incredible things with little or no effort. But now my normal has changed. And after struggling with that fact, I have finally reached the point where I understand that it is as normal as it gets.

Cancer changes your life forever. This does not mean that life is any less fulfilling or meaningful; it simply means that life is lived with a different perspective. Life now has become more intentional and more meaningful. Cancer causes you to see everything differently. Cancer causes you to appreciate the small things—a day without a nap, a day without pain, a day when you don't think about being sick, or a day that appears like the prior normal you were used to. But most of the time cancer causes you to accept a new normal and to appreciate it as God's gift and faithfulness.

There are days when I don't want to accept this new normal in my life. In fact, the longer I am a survivor, I have forgotten what it was like before cancer. Did I ever really walk right? Was there ever a time when I did not have pain? Did I really look like that? These thoughts continue to come to me late at night and in my quiet melancholy moments. But they are quickly chased away by thoughts of gratefulness and thanksgiving at being alive. God never changes but life with God is a life full of transformation. And transformation is God-directed change. While I do not believe that cancer is of God, I believe that God has used my cancer to transform me in ways that have been a blessing to me and to others. My perspective on health has been transformed. Now I see how valuable our health is and what an awesome gift "good health" is. While I sometimes struggle with this new "normal," I always find myself feeling extremely blessed to know that each day the possibility of complete healing becomes a reality for me.

Dear Lord, thank you for your grace and mercy that strengthen us day by day. Thank you for meeting us at the point of our needs right now. Thank you for comforting us in our present state of healing. Lord, thank you for your reassuring presence that lifts us and gives us the courage to live in this present reality in our lives. Amen.

Joining My Sisters

IT TOOK ME A WHILE TO ACCEPT THE FACT THAT I WAS A SURVIVOR. It took even longer to accept the fact that I needed to join with my sisters in the fight against breast cancer. I never knew how many African American women were affected by breast cancer until my diagnosis became known. It was then that I found out that many women I knew throughout the city were survivors. This list of survivors included women of all educational backgrounds, all denominations, all ages, all races, and a variety of careers. Many came to share their stories with me personally. Many were referred by others and some became known through conversations with friends and acquaintances. Gradually I realized that I belonged to a vast network of women who were cancer survivors who understood on a personal level what I was going through.

One of my high-school classmates who is a member of the church where I pastor and is a 17-year cancer survivor was one of the first women to share her story. Her quiet presence in church every Sunday was a constant reminder that God is a healer. Along with my mother-in-law, God placed before me women who shared their testimonies of faith in the face of cancer. The network of women kept growing and growing and it spread throughout the country. The sisterhood that was developed was a tremendous blessing to me.

I was totally floored when my dear friend, Reverend Delores McQuinn, came to inform me that I was being honored by the Sisters Network Central Virginia, Inc. as a role model during their annual Black History Month Program. Honored for what? For staying alive? I was humbled but convicted to become a part of this group of woman who so lovingly and courageously keep us abreast of how we as women can take better care of ourselves. It was at the program that I learned of all the wonderful things they do to walk with women before, during, and after cancer. I knew that this was a group to which I needed to belong.

Every year when we lift breast cancer before the congregation, I ask for my sisters and brothers who are breast cancer survivors to come forth for prayer. And every year I am reminded that this is a group I did not ask to join but life has made me a member of. And now that I am a member, I have to put my heart, mind, and spirit into the work. I ask God to use my testimony to be a blessing to someone else.

Dear Lord, bless all of my sisters and brothers who are breast cancer survivors. Thank you for their testimonies of faith that have encouraged others to not give up hope. Please bless the work of the Sisters Network for the awesome ministry they provide to women and men throughout this country. Give them the needed resources to continue this valuable work. Amen.

Another Chance

I HAVE ANOTHER CHANCE. Nothing makes that statement come alive more than having a bout with cancer. Surviving cancer helps you to know that every day gives us another chance—another chance to get it right, another chance to undo the wrong, another chance to do better, another chance to be better, another chance to complete our God-given assignment. I am ecstatic that God has given me another chance!

It's amazing how being a cancer survivor can help you realize that many things you have taken for granted are true. It is true that every day is a new day of promise and opportunity. It is true that every day gives us another chance to live life to its fullest and to be a better person. I am so grateful for another chance. I don't know what lies ahead but I do know that every day is blessed.

When I was an elementary school principal in Goochland County, one of the custodians would always let me know she was leaving with the parting words: *I'll see you tomorrow, Lord willing.* I certainly understood what she meant, but I felt it was unnecessary to always add the "Lord willing" part. But now as I look back, I wonder if, like me, she had experienced something in her life that made her keenly aware that tomorrow is not promised and that it is by the grace of God that we see each new day. When we awake and find ourselves in the land of the living, as the older saints like to say, it is because the Lord is willing to extend our time down here.

God gave me another chance. I still find myself wrestling with that fact. Why did I get another chance and others so much more deserving did not? Did I get another chance because I needed another chance to finish something or to undo something or to get something right or to undo some wrong or to finally understand what my purpose is here on earth? Another chance causes you to ponder and to wonder. What does another chance mean?

I have another chance and I'm grateful. I finally had to stop trying to figure out why and to embrace this gift that God has given me. I hope I don't squander this new opportunity that God has given me. I want to love more deeply and to be more forgiving and to finish the work that God has placed in my hands. I wake up each day grateful, but I also wake up a little scared because I don't want to mess up this new chance that God has given me. I want God to be pleased with God's decision to allow me more time.

Dear Lord, thank you for another chance. Thank you for allowing me more time to serve you and to love others. Bless all of those who have been given another chance because of your grace and mercy. Help us to find our purpose in you. Each day may our lives bring glory and honor to your name. Amen.

Survivor or Conqueror?

AT A CERTAIN TIME, AFTER FIVE YEARS, YOU GET TO BE CALLED A *CANCER SURVIVOR*. When I first heard that and began to refer to myself as a cancer survivor, it was great. It meant that I had survived the time period that most people deem as critical. It meant I could go on with my life. But as I dealt with my new status as a cancer survivor, I was confronted with what the Word had to say about my being a conqueror. The Word said that not only was I a conqueror but I am *more than a conqueror*. And there is a difference between being a survivor and a conqueror.

I have met survivors before. Many of them have a marvelous testimony and their stories are encouraging and inspiring. But I have also met the survivors who came through not better but bitter; not joyful but full of self-pity; not loving God but distant from God. They had survived the cancer but they had allowed cancer to conquer their spirits and their joy and their very being. They were survivors but not conquerors.

God promises that in whatever state we find ourselves, we can be more than conquerors through Christ Jesus. I was determined to live that scripture. I decided that while in my body I am a survivor, in my soul I am a conqueror. I decided to not allow cancer to rob me of the inner peace and joy that belongs to me. Each day I tell cancer to get behind me and to release me from any lingering thoughts of sadness and self-pity. I wake up each day declaring that I have conquered the power of cancer to limit my possibilities, my hopes, and my dreams.

I remember reading a poem about what cancer cannot do. I smile because I know that it's truth: cancer can only do what we allow it to do. The gospel or good news about cancer is that cancer reminds you of who is really in control. Cancer reminds me that I serve a God who has the power to heal, restore, and renew me in spite of the cancer.

Am I a survivor or a conqueror? I'm both! I am a cancer survivor who each day lives as a conqueror. Each day I live into what God has in store for me. It's not what I've survived; it's what I am able to conquer by the power of God's abundant grace.

Dear Lord, thank you for making us more than conquerors through your Son, Jesus Christ. Thank you for allowing us to survive the life-threatening effects of cancer in our bodies. Thank you for allowing us to face each day with the hope and trust that we will be more than conquerors. Amen.

5 Years!

IT'S HARD TO BELIEVE THAT IT'S BEEN FIVE YEARS SINCE I WAS DIAGNOSED WITH CANCER. As I got past "living" with cancer, I gradually stopped focusing on the time. And so as I stand at the five-year mark, I'm both surprised and overwhelmed. Five years is a long time. A lot happens and does not happen in five years. When I look back at the last five years, I realize a lot has changed for me over these years.

In the last five years I have lost some key family members and friends. In the last five years my mother has been diagnosed with severe dementia and along with my brother, I have become her primary caregiver. In the last five years, my brother's health has taken a turn and he now faces retiring on disability. As I reflect, I realize that I have had to deal with a lot of challenging things, things that challenged me emotionally and spiritually. But I also realize that I have a lot to celebrate.

It's been five years! And in these five years, a lot of good stuff has happened. In these five years, I have seen my beautiful daughter graduate from Deep Run High School, seen her off to Hampton University, and now I look forward to seeing her graduate in May with honors. God has been gracious to allow me to continue to work at both the church and the university. My husband and I have celebrated the 20-year milestone in our marriage. In these five years, the church has grown and we have been able to do awesome ministry together. In five years, we have moved into a new church facility back on the grounds of the original site. God has been awesome in these five years.

When I look back over where I started on this journey of "living" with cancer, I have a lot to celebrate. As the faithful, we often talk about *walking with God*, but often we miss the experience of what that actually means. In these five years, I have *walked with God* and have been awestruck at the fact that God has walked with me. God has been my constant companion along every turn and twist in the road. Each day, all day, every day, I have felt the overwhelming presence of God empowering me to take each step. It has been said that a journey starts with the first step. That first step with God has turned into FIVE YEARS!!

Dear Lord, thank you for this five-year celebration. Thank you for your abiding strength along the way. Bless all of those who need your assurance and abiding hope to continue the journey. Help all who need you today to make yet another step on this journey. Amen.

What Will Be My Legacy?

WHAT WILL BE MY LEGACY? That's the real question. Not what have I done. Not what name I made for myself. Not what degrees I've earned or what titles have been bestowed. What will be my legacy? What will people remember about me when I'm gone? What will be the focus of the conversations? What will be the remembered quotes? What will people want to model? What good thing will I have deposited in others? What will be my legacy?

Interestingly enough, when you are faced with your own mortality, material things never come to mind. Things that may have been important to you and others before don't even occupy space in your mind. What becomes critical is what you leave for others to build upon. I want to leave a legacy of faith that will bless women and others who suffer with life-threatening diseases. I want to leave a legacy of faith that with allow others to do the work that God has created them to do in spite of their present reality. I want to leave a legacy of faith that encourages others to stand up and to face each new day with courage and conviction and trust God to do the rest.

As I look back over my life, especially this journey with God during my illness, I pray that my legacy will be one of faith, commitment, and love. I cannot say enough about the role that faith has played in my life. I don't really remember all of how I came to trust God for living. I believe it had something to do with having my mother be deathly ill when I was a young girl and having my family dress me up to visit her for the last time, only to experience her complete healing. Perhaps it was watching how my parents approached the hardships of life with such love for one another, with laughter, and with an abiding sense of peace in the home. Perhaps it was the many church people who loved and laughed and worked together to make life wonderful as I grew up. They left me such a wonderful legacy of pride and determination and a positive self-esteem.

I want my legacy to be one of positive energy. I want to leave a legacy of love, unconditional love, ever-forgiving love, extravagant love, kind and gentle love. I want my legacy to be that I made people feel good and I left people better after they met me.

I realize that what I want my legacy to be may be far from what it would be if I died right now. I feel the weight of coming up short when it comes to leaving a legacy of love and hope and encouragement. Oh, I know people will always say kind things about you when you're gone. But I want what people say to be true. But more than that, I want people to have a desire to reproduce what they saw in me. I want to leave the kind of love and positive energy that can be reproduced in the lives of my husband and daughter, my family and friends, my church, my colleagues, my community, and even this world. What will be my legacy? I don't know, but thanks to God, each day provides an opportunity for me to make it one that will be pleasing to God. I still have time . . .

Dear Lord, thank you for reminding me that I have been created to deposit into the lives of others. Help us to live in such a way that others may find true life in you. Lord, create in each of us a legacy of faith and love that will bless the lives of others and give honor and glory to your name. Amen.

I Plan to Live Until I Die!

I PLAN TO LIVE UNTIL I DIE! I can no longer worry about what is. I can no longer spend time worrying about what I can no longer do. I can no longer wait to do what I have to do. Sick or well, there comes a time when we have to decide to live. There comes a time when we have to decide to press on and to go on in spite of the challenges. Whether cancer or not, life is full of challenges. Each day we are faced with things that bring us extreme joy or severe sorrow. And just as painful are the moments in between when we're in between good and bad, in between joy and sorrow, and in between full and empty. I have decided to live. Today, I declare: *I plan to live until I die!*

It's amazing how our words have power over our lives. We can either speak life or we can speak death over ourselves. And we do this on a daily basis. On a daily basis we speak defeat, sorrow, disappointment, weakness, confusion, and anxiety. We spiritually beat up on ourselves as a part of our daily routine and wonder why our spirits are downcast and broken. But the real danger is not just in what we speak, but in what we fail to speak that can give life and give us the power to live abundantly. We have to declare some things to ourselves and to others. And today, I declare: *I plan to live until I die!*

I have to declare this so that my body and my spirit will get on board. I have to declare this so that when I wake up each morning I will present myself as one who is ready and willing to live. There was a period in my illness when I did not present myself each day as one who was ready and willing to live. I presented myself as one who was not sure; I presented myself as one who was willing to give the decision to my cancer and allow my body to determine how I would experience each new day. But I have decided that some decisions I can make by the power of God that is in me. God has not given me a spirit of fear and so I don't have to fear living. *I plan to live until I die!*

As I was reading Psalm 118:17, it reminded me to stand firm on my declaration to live and not die. The psalmist makes this declaration after he reflects on all that God has done on his behalf and all that God promises to do in the future. And it is with the same joy that even though I realize that my journey is in no way over, I can plant my faith feet in the path called healing. So I can say with an assurance: *I plan to live until I die!* Until God says something different, I plan to live a life pleasing to God. Until I die, I plan to be faithful to the things God has placed in my hands to do. Until I die, I plan to not give up. And I plan to do this so that I can be a testimony to the goodness of the Lord in the land of the living. *I plan to live until I die* so that all might know what an awesome God I serve!

Dear Lord, thank you for each new day. Thank you for calling us to live each new day in the fullness of your spirit. As survivors, keep us focused on you that we may live and not die. Each day, help us to walk in the newness of life. In you, there is renewed hope and strength and we are so grateful. Thank you for your abiding presence in our lives. Amen.

 The Reverend Dr. Patricia A. Gould-Champ has served faithfully as the Pastor and Founding Visionary of the Faith Community Baptist Church in Richmond, Virginia, for the past nineteen years. Her thirty-two-year ministry career has focused on service to the least and the left out. The overwhelming goal and desire of her preaching and teaching is that people be saved, delivered, and empowered to live as God's people in this world. Through her leadership, Faith Community Baptist Church continues to serve the communities of Fairfield, Whitcomb, and Creighton Courts in the East End of the City of Richmond, Virginia, through such staple outreach ministries as the Tuesday Feeding Ministry, Spring Bible Camp, and the R.I.S.E. (Respect, Integrity, Success, and Empowerment) Women's Empowerment Group, a 24-week intimate focus group for the women in Fairfield, Whitcomb, and Creighton Courts.

Dr. Gould-Champ is a national facilitator in the area of HIV/AIDS Prevention Education, training churches and religious organizations to serve those infected and affected with the disease. This work has been recognized and funded by the Virginia Department of Health since 1995. With the diagnosis of her mother with dementia, Dr. Gould-Champ has become a facilitator and workshop leader, developing strategies to assist the families and loved ones of persons living with dementia.

Academically, Dr. Gould-Champ holds an earned doctorate from Virginia Polytechnic Institute and State University and received her Master of Divinity degree, *summa cum laude*, from the Samuel DeWitt Proctor School of Theology at Virginia Union University, where she has served as an Assistant Professor of Practical Theology for the past twenty years. Her seminary senior sermon entitled "An Unfinished Agenda" is published in Ella

Mitchell's book *Those Preaching Women, Volume II*, and her essay "Women and Preaching: Telling the Story in Our Own Voice" is featured in *Born to Preach: Essays in Honor of the Ministry of Henry and Ella Mitchell*. Her first published book, *Pamela Goes to Church*, a worship resource for children, is being used by churches throughout the country.

Dr. Gould-Champ was elected as the 35th and first female president of the Baptist General Convention of Virginia in 2003 and recently completed a one-year appointment as a member of the Interim Executive Minister Team responsible for Staff and Office Operations. She is a former Moderator of the Shiloh Baptist Association of Virginia and in 1995 received the YWCA Woman of the Year designation in the area of Religion.

Dr. Gould-Champ is supported in ministry by her beloved mother, Dorothy C. Gould, her life and ministry partner, James Champ, III, the president of Coordinated Insurance Services, and her precious daughter, Pamela Ann Champ, an honors graduate of Hampton University and an Audit Associate at KPMG, a Big Four Accounting Firm. In spite of Dr. Gould-Champ's adversities, she has modeled what it means to "walk by faith" and has stood firm in her belief that "without faith, it is impossible to please God."

www.ingramcontent.com/pod-product-compliance
Lightning Source LLC
Chambersburg PA
CBHW071225090426
42736CB00014B/2972